# LAKE INVADERS

# GREAT LAKES BOOKS

EDITOR
Thomas Klug, Marygrove College

A complete listing of the books in this series can
be found online at wsupress.wayne.edu

# LAKE INVADERS

## INVASIVE SPECIES AND THE BATTLE
## FOR THE FUTURE OF THE GREAT LAKES

### WILLIAM RAPAI

Wayne State University Press
Detroit

20 19 18 17 16      5 4 3 2 1

ISBN 978-0-8143-4124-7 (paperback)
ISBN 978-0-8143-4125-4 (ebook)

Library of Congress Cataloging Number:
2015958674

*Designed and typeset by Bryce Schimanski*
*Composed in Adobe Caslon Pro*

*To my father, the old fisherman*
*He may be gone, but fish still tremble at his name*

# CONTENTS

# ACKNOWLEDGMENTS

The best thing about a project like this is the ability to meet interesting people who are doing cool things. In the course of writing this book, I've interviewed more than a hundred people from the United States and Canada, and I can honestly say I have not met one that I didn't like.

It would be impossible for me to list all the people and thank them individually, so let me just issue a blanket statement: Thank you all. I appreciate everything you've done for me. I appreciate your guidance, your answers, your thoughts, your frankness, your effort, and your time.

Nevertheless, I must thank a few people in particular for their special contributions:

Erika Jensen for your patience and competence, and for never running away when you saw me coming.

Sarah LeSage and David Reid for keeping me from drowning in ballast water.

Mike Hoff for your dedication, insight, and good humor.

Lindsay Chadderton for answering my dumb questions with a smile and not a smirk.

And finally to David Jude for reminding me that there's still wonder in the world around me, and it's okay to get excited about it.

The biggest thank-yous go to my family. To Maggie and Julia, thank you for keeping me on my toes, for being patient, for helping me to keep perspective, and for not losing faith in your old dad. Of course, the biggest thank-you of all goes to The Lovely Joann. I appreciate you looking over my shoulder, keeping me on track, and giving me inspiration every day. Instead of forcing me to take a soul-crushing job in a windowless cubicle, you have allowed me to go off on two quixotic journeys that, well, haven't provided much help when it comes to paying the bills. But for giving me the freedom to explore and follow my curiosity, I shall always be grateful.

# INTRODUCTION

Lurking in the murky brown-gray water of an Illinois river, just fifty-five miles from Lake Michigan, is a swarm of creatures so scary, so disgusting, that many people want them exterminated.

They're slimy and ugly. They jump at the approach of humans, and if one hits you, it could break your nose. They breed like crazy, capable of producing millions and millions of offspring in a single year. Once you have them, you can't get rid of them; despite their huge population, they are hard to find and hard to catch. And they're hungry. They are so hungry in fact that they're stripping rivers clean of food, and biologists fear what these hungry beasts could do if they were to reach the Great Lakes.

While these carps—these vandals at the gates—receive massive attention, other invasive species have been attacking, doing massive damage to the Great Lakes for seventy years, often without notice. More than 180 exotic species are in the Great Lakes. Some, such as green algae, the Asian tapeworm, and the suckermouth minnow, have had little or no impact so far. But a handful of others—sea lamprey, alewife, round goby, quagga mussel, zebra mussel, Eurasian watermilfoil, spiny water flea, and rusty crayfish—have conducted an all-out assault on the Great Lakes and are winning the battle. In the process, they have changed the populations of native fish and planktons. They've changed water clarity and water chemistry. They've changed the food web and the nutrient cycle.

The carps? In reality, if they were to enter the Great Lakes, they would only be shooting the wounded.

Of course, we humans are not aquatic animals, so the changes occurring as a result of these introductions are not something we can easily see. But if we lived under the surface of the water, we would be shocked by what we see today: strange and foreign creatures now have prominent positions in the Great Lakes ecosystem, including a fish with a hundred teeth arranged in a terrifying whorl and a tiny crustacean with a barbed sword for a tail.

1

For centuries, the Great Lakes were safe from these outsiders. The flow of water from Lake Ontario down the St. Lawrence River to the ocean kept floating organisms from entering. Any fish that was able to fight its way into Lake Ontario could not pass the impenetrable wall of Niagara Falls. But the lakes' natural protection was compromised in the eighteenth century with the opening of the Welland Canal, a waterway in southern Ontario that gave aquatic species—as well as vessels—a path around the falls. Then, in 1959, rapids on the St. Lawrence River were bypassed with the opening of a system of locks that gave foreign organisms access to the farthest reaches of the Great Lakes.

Many of those organisms entered the Great Lakes in the ballast tanks of international ships—freighters that might as well have been floating aquariums, transporting organisms from Europe, South America, or Asia along with their cargoes. As those ships traveled through the Great Lakes and stopped in ports, they discharged the water that they had taken in elsewhere—water that helped the ships stay balanced as they crossed oceans. Animals, bacteria, and viruses from all over the world, welcome to your new home.

————

Not all the species that have been introduced to the Great Lakes are "invasive." In fact, most of the new species in the lakes aren't considered invasive because they have not had visible or measurable impacts on the ecosystem. An organism is considered to be "exotic" if it somehow finds its way into an area beyond its native range or region. Although there are no hard and fast rules, three things can happen to exotics when they enter a new environment.

- They can die out because they cannot adapt to the climate and conditions or have no way to reproduce. Perhaps the organisms need salt or brackish water. Perhaps there are predators that will eliminate them before they can become established. Perhaps they can't survive the frigid temperatures of winter or the relatively cold water of a temperate climate. In fact, very few introduced species will survive in the Great Lakes.

- They can spread benignly but have almost no impact on their new ecosystem.

- Or perhaps they can find a comfortable ecological niche and become invasive. A species is considered to be invasive when it spreads rapidly and has a huge impact, harming native species, altering the food web, and changing the very nature of its new ecosystem.

The Great Lakes have always been dynamic. Fish populations and water levels have fluctuated over centuries, but prior to European settlement, change was slow, which allowed the lakes and organisms time to adapt. The pace of change began to accelerate in the eighteenth century as humans began to remove huge numbers of fish. The pace of change accelerated in the mid-twentieth century as growing human populations used the Great Lakes as a dumping ground for their human and industrial wastes. The arrival of invasive species, however, has further quickened the pace of change. The round goby was discovered in the St. Clair River in 1990, and only twenty-two years later, there were an estimated 9.9 billion of them in Lake Erie alone. All those gobies have had a profound effect on native fish populations. Zebra mussels were discovered in 1988 and quagga mussels in 1989, and only twenty-five years later, it was estimated there were 450 trillion quagga and zebra mussels in Lake Michigan alone. Those two mussels have consumed massive amounts of plankton, causing a crash in the Great Lakes food web that has led to the extirpation and perhaps the extinction of some zooplankton species.

The damage doesn't end at the shoreline. The Great Lakes have been the beachhead for the invasion of several species that have spread across North America. The zebra mussel, for example, was discovered in the Great Lakes in 1988, but only three years later, it was already in lakes in Kentucky and tributaries that flow into the Mississippi River. In 2007, zebra mussels were found in the Colorado River in Arizona, and by 2011, they had spread into more than half the United States, including lakes and rivers in Texas, North Dakota, Utah, and Colorado and in Canada from Manitoba east to Nova Scotia.

———

The Great Lakes stretch for 750 miles on a straight line from Duluth, Minnesota, on the west to Montreal, Quebec, on the east. They are one-fifth of the world's fresh surface water. They are a $7 billion fishery. Their watershed is home to more than thirty-five hundred species of plants and animals.

Even though the lakes are all part of one ecosystem, each one is an individual with its own characteristics and personality. Cold, deep, and huge, Lake Superior has very little in common with the shallow and relatively warm water of Lake Erie. Erie has only 2 percent of all the water in the Great Lakes, but it has 50 percent of all the fish. Conversely, Lake Superior has more than 50 percent of the water, but only 2 percent of the fish.[1] Some hydrologists consider Lakes Michigan and Huron to be just one big lake because they are connected at the Straits of Mackinac and are at the same elevation. But Lake Michigan is deep like a pot, and Lake Huron is shallow like a frying pan; and they differ dramatically in how much aquatic life they support. Lake Huron by itself can't even be considered its own big ecosystem, as the rocky shores and cold clear water of Georgian Bay have very little in common with the flat shores and shallow, warm water of Saginaw Bay.

Together, however, the Great Lakes are responsible for a thriving regional economy. If the Great Lakes basin were its own country, it would be the fourth-largest economy in the world, representing $62 billion in wages and more than $200 billion in economic activity annually. The lakes are responsible for more than five hundred thousand jobs in Michigan alone.[2]

But now invasive species are reshaping the lakes and the economy. The impact is often difficult to identify because more often than not the links are casual or circumstantial. But sometimes the link is clear. In 1989, zebra mussels helped to clog the water intake for the municipal water-treatment plant in Monroe, Michigan, forcing the plant to shut down and twenty-four thousand people to go without drinking water. The estimated cost to clean the pipes and make the plant operational was more than $300,000. A 2008 study estimated that invasives that entered the Great Lakes via ballast water from international shipping has resulted in $200 million in losses to the region's economy annually.[3]

What makes the situation worse is that biologists really don't know whether this is the worst of the damage to the Great Lakes or just the start. Invasion biology is a young field—nobody had ever used the term "invasive species" prior to 1990—and scientists are just starting to understand how introduced species affect ecosystems.

Despite this lack of knowledge, three things are clear to biologists:

- If an exotic species is able to establish a breeding population in the Great Lakes, eradication is impossible. The only option is to find a way to control the invader and limit the damage.

- The invasive species already in the Great Lakes are causing a massive, ongoing biological reorganization that's difficult for the general public to see and understand.

- There will be winners and losers among the native organisms, and the secret to being a winner will be adaptability—developing an appetite for nonnatives. That ability to adapt is paramount because the Great Lakes food web is now built on nonnative species.

Like the carps, other species are lurking, poised to do even more damage. The US Coast Guard has identified several hundred species in Europe, Asia, and

The sun sets over Lake Michigan at McGulpin Point Lighthouse, just west of the Mackinaw Bridge. On the surface, the lake hasn't changed much over the past seven thousand years. Under the surface, however, the lake is undergoing a major ecological reshuffling caused by invasive species.

South America that are threats to the Great Lakes because they currently live in a similar climate. Other animals that could do additional damage are much closer than you might think—in bait stores, pet shops, live food markets, and, believe it or not, classrooms.

To be clear, the issue surrounding invasive species is not whether we wish to prevent new species from entering the Great Lakes. The issue is protecting the diversity of life in the Great Lakes. Or, to look at it another way, the issue is preventing the lakes from becoming dominated by only a few superorganisms.

There, however, is new reason for hope and optimism. Despite these massive changes that have compromised the ecosystem, the Great Lakes are enduring and in some cases showing signs of recovery. Biologists and policy makers have opened several fronts in the war against invasives, and they are starting to grapple with the most pressing challenges. Multimillion-dollar commitments from both the US and Canadian governments are helping to fund research, prevention, and education efforts. Biologists have learned to control some invasives and are working on controls for others. For those organisms that are more difficult to control, the new goal is to look deep into their genetic makeup to search for weaknesses that can be exploited. New coalitions are developing prevention policies because reacting to invasive species once they are in the ecosystem is mostly ineffective, and there are considerable economic and biological advantages to stopping them before they arrive. Finally, biologists and policy makers are working to answer the most important, the most relevant questions about the impact of these organisms and to set a new baseline for measuring the health of the Great Lakes going forward. Even though the Great Lakes ecosystem is now significantly different from what it once was, it is still possible to set goals and develop strategies to protect what we still have and try to reverse some of the damage.

Certainly industrial pollution, agricultural runoff, climate change, and overfishing have also had impacts on the Great Lakes, so it would be wrong to think that invasive species are the only cause of change. This book, however, focuses on the impacts of invasives. The chapters delve into the ecological and economic damages that have occurred and are occurring and explore educational efforts and policies designed to prevent new introductions. Each chapter features the stories of the largely unnoticed and unrecognized people—the foot soldiers—who have committed themselves to slowing, stopping, and reversing the invasion and keeping the lakes resilient enough to absorb the inevitable attacks to come.

But before we can assess the profound changes that have occurred and determine exactly what has been lost, we need to look back and understand what made these lakes great.

# 1

# THE LAKES ARE CHANGED FOREVER

On the west wall of the Buffalo History Museum in Buffalo, New York, there is a bas-relief in the building's fresco, sculpted from Vermont marble, of four men: George Coit, Charles Townsend, Samuel Wilkeson, and DeWitt Clinton. The sculpture depicts a symbolic act during Buffalo's celebration of the opening of the Erie Canal on November 23, 1825—the pouring of water from the Atlantic Ocean into Lake Erie.

Only a few weeks before, on October 26, the Erie Canal opened to traffic, allowing for a flow of goods and people between New York City and the Great Lakes. The route took boats up the Hudson River to Albany and then west on the Mohawk River and the Erie Canal to Buffalo. The canal stretched more than 360 miles and became the first navigable route from the Atlantic Ocean to the upper Great Lakes. Even though the Great Lakes were connected to the Atlantic via the St. Lawrence River, two barriers made the flow of commerce and human migration difficult: rapids near Montreal and Niagara Falls.

The opening of the Erie Canal was a major engineering achievement, and the celebration was no small affair. As the celebration began, two kegs of Lake Erie water were loaded onto the packet boat *Seneca Chief*, which left the dock at ten a.m., pulled by four horses, bound for New York City. Following the *Seneca Chief* down the canal were four other barges, one of which, *Noah's Ark*, carried "a bear, two eagles, two fawns, several fish, and two Indian boys in the dress of their nation" for display in New York City from the places in the "west."[1]

On November 4, after several grand celebrations at towns along the canal and the Mohawk and Hudson Rivers, the boats sailed past New York City to Sandy Hook, New Jersey, and docked where the Hudson River meets the Atlantic Ocean.

In the ceremony at Sandy Hook, New York governor DeWitt Clinton dumped the Lake Erie water into the Atlantic Ocean in a ceremony dubbed "The Wedding of the Waters." The end of the ceremony meant that the wedding was complete, but it had yet to be consummated. So, early in the morning on November 23, the *Seneca Chief* arrived back in Buffalo on its return trip. Among the items in its cargo was a keg of water from the Atlantic Ocean.

At ten a.m., in another grand ceremony, Judge Samuel Wilkeson, one of Buffalo's biggest boosters, stepped onto the bow of the *Seneca Chief* and emptied the saltwater from the Atlantic into the sweet water of Lake Erie. It was only a symbolic act, but the Great Lakes had been changed forever.

––––

The Great Lakes are the youngest natural features in North America, attaining their current shapes and sizes only about eight thousand years ago. Name another natural feature—the Mississippi River, the Rocky Mountains, the Appalachian Mountains—and geology textbooks will tell you they were formed millions of years ago. The formation of the Great Lakes as we know them today began only fifteen thousand years ago, when the Wisconsin Glacier receded, but the geological underpinnings of the Great Lakes were laid more than 1.2 million years ago. The process began when two tectonic plates split and formed a river valley that became Lake Superior. Some five hundred million years later, a second tectonic shift formed river valleys that became Lakes Erie and Ontario and the St. Lawrence River. And then, five million years ago, the Ice Age began, and a series of glaciers moved across northern North America. The last in the series—the Wisconsin Glacier—pushed as far south as northern Pennsylvania and covered all of Michigan and most of Ohio, Illinois, Indiana, Wisconsin, and Minnesota. As the glaciers pushed south, withdrew back north, and pushed south again over thousands of years, their tremendous weight compressed the land underneath and pushed up the land in front of it, creating rock and soil formations at the glacier's boundaries.

No one knows the cause, but about fifteen thousand years ago, the climate began to warm and the Wisconsin Glacier started to melt and recede. The melting glacier left behind huge amounts of water, much of which was trapped between the moraines and the melting ice. This meltwater acted as a giant lake and set the stage for the first species to arrive in the Great Lakes basin—the animals and plants from the Mississippi River basin, areas south of the glacier, and the Atlantic Ocean. Those species—from the lake trout and walleye at the top of the food web to the smallest diatom at the bottom—adapted to the rapidly changing conditions of the Great Lakes basin and are now what we think of as native today.

With the St. Lawrence River blocked by ice and the surface of the land still compressed from the weight of the glaciers, huge amounts of meltwater flowed south through gaps in the moraines into the Maumee River in Ohio, which flowed southwest into the Wabash River in Indiana[2] and the Chicago River in Illinois. Both the Wabash and Chicago directed their water into the Mississippi River.[3] Soon, with the weight of the glacier removed, the land underneath began to rise in a process called crustal rebound. The lower water levels and the rebounding land caused the Wabash and Maumee Rivers to separate into two rivers, but before the land in northern Ontario could recover and rise, massive amounts of water flowed across central Ontario to the St. Lawrence River and the Atlantic Ocean.[4] That great flush took Great Lakes water levels so low that they were only about 10 percent of what they are today. Eventually, the combination of lower water levels and higher land blocked most of the drainage channels, and water backed up to allow the Great Lakes to reach modern levels.

Throughout this period, the organisms in the meltwater were sorting themselves out and forming the food web of the Great Lakes basin. The meltwater itself was too cold and lacked nutrients—nitrogen and phosphorous—to support a wide variety of life. Still, life in the Great Lakes began to take hold and flourish.

At one time, scientists thought that organisms—inside the Great Lakes and out—were part of a food "chain," with plants consumed by herbivores and carnivores consuming the herbivores in a one-way flow of nutrients from bottom to top. A more accurate description of the food web would be "what eats what" because food chains overlap, organisms on the same level consume each other, and even top predators are sometimes prey. Because the flow of nutrients isn't necessarily one way, Charles Darwin referred to it as a "web of complex relations" with organisms trying to outwit each other in a life-or-death game of survival. Because it's not simply a predator-prey relationship, it's more accurate to think of the organisms in the Great Lakes as being on five levels: producers, primary consumers, secondary consumers, top predators, and decomposers.

Plankton are among the organisms at the producer level and are the base of the food web. But not all plankton are equal. Phytoplankton—algae, dinoflagellates, and diatoms—are microscopic plants with no means of locomotion that obtain their energy from sunlight through photosynthesis and nutrients from phosphorous and nitrogen. The Great Lakes are lucky to have them. With the flow of meltwater away from the glacier, phytoplankton would never have been able to enter the Great Lakes since they move only with water flow. Fortunately for the Great Lakes, phytoplankton found a back door. At the time that the Great Lakes were forming, so was glacial Lake Agassiz. Now largely farmland and prairie, Lake Agassiz was at one time the largest known lake on Earth, covering parts of what is now North Dakota, Minnesota, Ontario, and Manitoba. Because water in Lake Agassiz flowed north, it drew the phytoplankton in from rivers that now drain to the Mississippi. As the glacier continued to recede, water in Lake Agassiz found a pathway into Ontario's Lake Nipigon, which drains into Lake Superior. Once in Superior, the phytoplankton spread into the other five lakes.

Another type of plankton—zooplankton—is tougher to define. Zooplankton are animals that may or may not be microscopic and may or may not have some elementary means of locomotion. Native zooplanktons include cladocerans (water fleas), copepods (oarsmen), and malacostrans (which includes *Diporeia*, which is rapidly disappearing in the Great Lakes). Even though zooplankton and phytoplankton are the basis of the food web, they are not closely related. There's also a major difference between the two groups: phytoplankton are producers, and zooplankton are primary and secondary consumers, as they may feed on phytoplankton or on other zooplankton. (The exotic freshwater jellyfish, which originated in China and can now be found in the Great Lakes, is an example of a nonmicroscopic zooplankton that feeds on other zooplankton.) Besides zooplankton, other primary consumers are tadpoles, crayfish, mayfly nymphs, crustaceans, and certain ducks.

Secondary consumers—the small fish in the middle that feed on plankton—can be both predator and prey.

The top predators of the Great Lakes settled in different temperature gradients, with lake trout dominating the colder regions and walleyes dominating the warmer lakes and bays. But even the top predators are prey occasionally for other aquatic species and for nonaquatic species such as herons, egrets, osprey, eagles, and humans.

Then there are the decomposers, which are the bacteria and organisms that live at the benthic layer—the bottom of the lake. They have their own place in the food web and have the thankless job of decomposing fecal matter and dead stuff and turning it back into nitrogen and phosphorous, which are nutrients for phytoplankton. Although we think of the phytoplankton as being the base of the food web, in reality it's phosphorous and nitrogen; without those two nutrients, there is no life.

Because there are far more streams that provide these nutrients at the southern end of the Great Lakes, southern Lake Michigan, Saginaw Bay, and Lake Erie are the areas with the most abundant life, or are what biologists refer to as "productive." Lake Erie is the most productive lake today and also was likely the most productive lake for fish prior to European settlement, as huge swamps on the southern and western part of the lake provided nutrients that supported the food web and acted as nurseries for small fish.

Worldwide, it's a rule of thumb that cold-water lakes and streams have fewer species than do warm-water lakes and streams, and the Great Lakes are no different. Although the Great Lakes contain organisms that were able to survive in the cold glacial runoff, those organisms are able to survive today because the lakes are in a temperate climate. Still, many of the species that are found in the Great Lakes would be unable to survive much farther to the south or in shallower water. And as the earth's climate continues to change, more warm-water species—specifically the yellow perch and walleye—are increasingly being found in Lake Huron, which previously had been the cold-water domain of whitefish and lake trout.

The combination of cold water and isolation means that the Great Lakes were ripe for invasion. Compare a spot in the Great Lakes to a spot in the Pacific Ocean with a similar temperature range and you will find far fewer species in the lakes; in the Pacific Ocean, there could be two thousand species, while in the Great Lakes, there could be twelve. The result of that lack of life in the Great Lakes meant that there would be multiple open niches for introduced organisms. Because the lakes were isolated, they were also vulnerable.

---

The construction of the Erie Canal meant the Great Lakes were now open to trade and new organisms. But the completion of this new water highway increased anxiety in the province of Upper Canada. Politicians and businesspeople from the north side of the Great Lakes saw the Erie Canal as a major economic and political threat and made the construction of a canal on the Canadian side a priority. Canadian businesspeople feared that the Erie Canal would divert the flow of trade into the interior of the continent from Montreal to New York City, and they wanted a trade route that was not subject to American whims.

Progress was already being made on opening a Canadian route from the Atlantic with the opening of the Lachine Canal in Montreal, just months before the Erie Canal opened. That canal provided a shipping route around rapids in the St. Lawrence River, but ships were limited by their size—only shallow-draft vessels could make it through additional rapids above Montreal. Once the ships reached Lake Ontario, they could only go so far because the three-hundred-foot Niagara Falls acted as a dead end. The only way around the falls was an expensive, time-consuming, and circuitous route: cargo that had come across Lake Ontario was unloaded at Lewiston, New

York, and moved over land to a spot near Buffalo above Niagara Falls, where it was loaded on another ship for the remainder of the journey to frontier towns and forts. This gave the new Erie Canal significant advantages over the St. Lawrence / Lake Ontario route: it was quicker and cheaper, and it was able to stay open longer in the autumn and open earlier in the spring. Prior to the opening of the Erie Canal, wheat grown in western New York took twenty days to reach Albany by wagon, and it cost one hundred dollars to move a ton. Via the canal, a ton of wheat could be shipped to New York City in just ten days for only five dollars.[5] Since each boat could carry twenty-five tons, the cost savings were considerable.

In an effort to protect the Canadian trade route, the legislature of Upper Canada moved swiftly to authorize the construction of a twenty-seven-mile canal with forty locks that would allow ships to make their way more than three hundred feet up the Niagara Escarpment and pass between Lake Ontario and Lake Erie.

The Welland Canal was opened on November 30, 1829, as the schooner *Anne & Jane* nosed its way into the first lock for the two-day voyage from Lake Ontario to Lake Erie. The canal was both bigger and better than the Erie Canal, as it was capable of handling schooners that could carry more than one hundred tons of freight. Finished goods could now be shipped cheaply and efficiently from ports on the East Coast or from Europe to young, fast-growing cities on the Great Lakes, and the natural resources of the frontier—iron ore, copper, fish, grain, lumber—could be shipped back.

The canal was the vision of William Hamilton Merritt, a businessman in the Niagara Peninsula who bought a run-down sawmill and a gristmill on Twelve Mile Creek near St. Catharines, Ontario. Unfortunately for Merritt, he discovered that at certain times of the year—especially in the late summer—there was a shortage of water to power his mills. Merritt began to explore ways to divert water from the nearby Welland River atop the Niagara Escarpment, the rock formation that forms Niagara Falls. But as Merritt considered his options for water diversion, he realized that he was looking at a route for a canal that would bypass Niagara Falls.

Construction of the Welland Canal took five years, and shortly after it opened, Merritt concluded that it was a money-losing venture. In just a few months, the government stepped in and built a larger canal nearby, making Merritt's canal obsolete. Even though Merritt lost control of the Welland Canal, he refused to give up on the idea of unimpeded trade between Europe and cities on the Great Lakes. Before he died in 1862, he circulated a pamphlet that called for a series of locks to be built along the St. Lawrence River that would allow ships to bypass the rapids that prevented the flow of trade from the Atlantic through the Welland

Canal and into the upper Great Lakes. Powerful business interests in the United States successfully blocked the construction of locks on the St. Lawrence River for more than one hundred years. But finally, in 1959, the locks were completed and the St. Lawrence Seaway opened. But even without the St. Lawrence Seaway, the combination of the Erie, Welland, and Lachine Canals opened a trade artery between the Atlantic Ocean and Toronto, Buffalo, Detroit, Milwaukee, and Chicago—ports on a burgeoning frontier.

---

The opening of the two canals brought millions of people into the heart of the continent. With the War of 1812 over, European settlers in North America began to move west and settle the Great Lakes basin in large numbers. Along the way, settlers stripped the land of great forests and filled in wetlands along the shoreline to make way for agriculture. In 1850, the population of Chicago was only about thirty thousand. By 1900, the population had grown to almost 1.7 million.

All these new people put new stresses on the Great Lakes. The vast waters were seen not only as a great source of food and water for drinking and industry; they were also seen as a place to easily dispose of human and industrial wastes. Mining, agriculture, and lumbering in the late 1800s changed the nature of erosion and the flow of nutrients and sediments into rivers and the lakes. Dam building for electrical power prevented fish from being able to migrate up channels to spawn and changed the nature of the streams by creating reservoirs and causing the water behind the dams to warm, rendering the streams uninhabitable to many cold-water fish species. Agriculture and urban expansion filled in coastal wetlands that were critical to absorbing pollutants that flowed in from the land. Nutrient levels in the Great Lakes from human waste and agricultural runoff increased, turning Lake Erie in particular into a giant algae bed on top and an oxygen-starved layer on the bottom. Although many biologists believe an oxygen-starved layer existed at the bottom of Lake Erie prior to European settlement, there's no question that the additional nutrient flow into the Great Lakes has made the layer larger.

In the mid-twentieth century, PCBs, DDT, lead, mercury, and other heavy metals were reaching critical levels. Fish in several areas of the Great Lakes were rendered inedible for humans because they contained unsafe levels of mercury. Ducks in the Detroit River and Lake St. Clair died from petroleum waste dumped in the water. In Cleveland, the joke was that if a person fell in the Cuyahoga River, he wouldn't drown—he would decompose.

At the same time, those areas of the Great Lakes that were less affected by pollution—Lake Superior, Lake Huron, and northern Lake Michigan—were seeing fish stocks quickly depleted by overfishing. In 1926, which was considered the peak year of the Great Lakes commercial fishery, twelve thousand people were employed in the industry. And although the value of the annual catch varied little over the next four decades, abundance changed considerably, as did the species being caught. When one species of fish disappeared, commercial fishers simply switched to another—until that one was also gone.[6] Among the biggest losses was the blue pike, a walleye subspecies that evolved in Lakes Erie and Ontario and once numbered in the millions. (Fishing depleted blue pike stocks, but it was likely the impact of the invasive rainbow smelt that finished it off.)

Despite all of this bad news, something else was happening in the Great Lakes basin: Following World War II, there was an explosion in the number of middle-class Americans and Canadians with leisure time. They bought powerboats and went fishing. They bought shotguns and went duck hunting. They bought sailboats and went cruising. And, quite unintentionally, they turned into environmentalists. This new group became upset by what they saw happening to the water quality of the Great Lakes—the ducks dying by the millions, the fish too contaminated to eat, oil slicks stretching for miles—and they demanded change. Politicians on both sides of the border heeded their demands to curb the flow of pollution into the lakes, and federal, state, and provincial governments passed new laws to limit the input.

But just as these pollution controls were starting to show their value and the Great Lakes were showing signs of recovery, two invaders from the Atlantic touched off yet another environmental calamity.

2

# THE NEW NORMAL

The East Shore Marina on the east side of Betsie Lake is an idyllic spot. On the north side of the lake is Frankfort, Michigan, a town that has evolved over the years to cater to boaters, tourists, and anglers. The south side of the lake is lined with summer homes and the village of Elberta. In the distance, at the west side of Betsie Lake, is the opening to Lake Michigan and what has been for decades some of the best sport fishing in the Great Lakes.

Even though it's mid-June and school is out, there's practically no one around, and the docks are less than two-thirds full of boats.

At the end of one dock, Jason Rusch works on the boat *Family Feud*, a forty-foot Silverton that belongs to his father. As Rusch stows his gear and minds his daughter and dog, he recounts the days when he had a captain's license and could make good money on a fishing trip. "There used to be a lot of money doing it," Rusch says. "Not so much these days."

It used to be that a charter captain could work only part of the year and make a good living. The season would start with walleye charters in Lake Erie, and by midsummer, it would move to Lake Michigan for coho and chinook salmon and rainbow trout.

Rusch's dad started as a charter-boat captain in the 1980s, first in Ludington, then here in Frankfort. In high school and college, Rusch helped his dad until he got his own captain's license and would then take out charters on his dad's boat or on other boats when their captains were unavailable. For just a few short weeks every summer, he could make $8,000—not bad money for a student, he says.

Rusch doesn't run charters anymore, and now that his dad is retired, the boat is strictly for recreation. As the sole supporting parent of a young daughter, Rusch has to have steady work, so he's taken a job in construction.

15

Charter fishing boats at Frankfort, Michigan, marina. The number of fishing charters is on the decline as Lake Michigan salmon are declining in both size and numbers, reflecting changes in the lake's food web caused by invasive species.

And he's not alone. Now, he says, pretty much every captain has to have a part-time job as a builder or electrician, snowplow operator, or something else. For charter fishing captains, this is the new normal.

Charter captains now need a second job because there just isn't the demand to go fishing like there used to be. The demand isn't there because there are fewer trophy fish out in the lake than there used to be. There are far fewer trophy fish because there are far fewer little fish to feed the big fish. The reason there are far fewer little fish is simple: the alewife population crashed in 2004.

The alewife was one of the first invasive species in the Great Lakes, entering about the same time as the sea lamprey, a parasitic fish. The lamprey quickly spread, all but eliminating the lakes' top predators—lake trout and whitefish—two species that also happened to be the most profitable for commercial fishermen.

The alewife, meanwhile, a small, otherwise unremarkable fish, bided its time. But once the lamprey all but eliminated the lake trout, the alewife took advantage of the vacuum—the absence of the lakes' apex predator—to expand its population to breathtaking numbers in Lakes Michigan and Huron.

Even though the sea lamprey and the alewife did not collude, it's impossible to tell the story of one without telling the story of the other, because the impacts of their arrivals are still rippling through the lakes today.

———

The Europeans who settled on the shores of the Great Lakes believed the supply of fish was inexhaustible. Commercial fishing on the Great Lakes began in the late eighteenth century and grew rapidly. Fish not only made a big part of the diet of the growing population in the Great Lakes basin; the catch was sent to markets in fast-growing cities on the East Coast. Lake sturgeon, one of the oldest fish species on Earth, was plentiful, but the bony fish wasn't thought of as food. Instead, sturgeon were brought on shore and fed to pigs or dried and then burned as fuel in Great Lakes steamboats.

Not surprisingly, the fish stocks were indeed exhaustible. Lake whitefish, which was considered the "deer of the lakes" for its tastiness, was the first species to crash. In 1846, the combined catch between the ports of Alpena and Presque Isle, Michigan, supplied 15 percent of all the fish caught by commercial fisheries on both sides of the Great Lakes. By the late 1800s, fish stocks in this section of Lake Huron were on the decline as a result of overfishing but also because of the impact of the lumber industry. The process of driving logs down rivers in Michigan, Ontario, and Wisconsin tore up river bottoms, which disrupted whitefish spawning areas. Then sawdust from the lumbering and sawmills began coating river bottoms, deoxygenizing the water. Commercial fishermen saw whitefish stocks plummet so quickly that the harvest went from more than twenty-four million pounds in 1879 to just nine million pounds in 1899.

Once whitefish were exhausted, commercial fishers turned to lake trout, and the result was the same. According to research cited by the US Geological Survey, "The commercial fishing industry was seeing their industry evaporate right before their eyes. In the ten years between 1937 and 1947, the lake trout harvest went from 3.4 million pounds to virtually nothing. In Lake Michigan, catch fell from 5.5 million pounds in 1946 to 402 pounds in 1953."[1] One reason for the dramatic drop in fish stocks was consistent lack of management and oversight. Because the US Constitution does not specifically address fisheries, states immediately assumed responsibilities for the Great Lakes under the Tenth Amendment. That meant that from Duluth to the St. Lawrence River, responsibility for the health of the lakes was controlled by Minnesota, Wisconsin, Illinois, Indiana, Michigan, Ohio, Pennsylvania, New York, Ontario, and Quebec, which was an arrangement that ensured a complex relationship. The jurisdictions not only refused to coordinate; they occasionally set regulations that conflicted.

A second reason for the dramatic drop in fish stocks was World War II. During the war, the US government asked the commercial fishing industry to overfish to supply food for the war effort.

A third reason for the drop in the fish population, particularly among the large apex predators, was the arrival of the invasive sea lamprey.

The sea lamprey (*Petromyzon marinus*) is among the oldest living creatures on Earth. It's also among the ugliest. Even though the sea lamprey looks like an eel—long and thin with no real fins—it's still a fish. It has two tiny eyes, its gills are a series of holes behind its head, and it can grow to be nearly three feet long. It's strange enough to look at in the hand or an aquarium, but a close look at its suction-cup mouth reveals a terrifying yet fascinating whorl of more than one hundred teeth made of keratin. These teeth grab onto a fish and scrape away the scales while its sharp tongue digs deeper to suck out blood and other fluids.

Nick Johnson, a research ecologist with the US Geological Survey's Hammond Bay Biological Station in northeastern Michigan, admits that the sea lamprey's looks help to mold public support for control. "If it looked like a koala bear, we might have some issues," Johnson says.

The sea lamprey was historically found in the North Atlantic from North America to Europe and into the Mediterranean Sea, and some biologists argue that the sea lamprey is native to Lake Ontario—a remnant of the Pleistocene Era, when saltwater covered the Great Lakes. Other biologists believe the sea lamprey entered Lake Ontario in the 1830s from the Erie Canal through a connecting waterway.[2] But there's one thing that everyone agrees on: the lamprey was not native to the lakes above Niagara Falls.

Biologists believe the sea lamprey found its way into Lake Erie in the early 1930s after improvements were made to the Welland Canal in 1919. Once the lamprey made it past the locks, it quickly spread and was discovered in Lake Michigan in 1936, Lake Huron in 1937, and Lake Superior in 1938.

Four lamprey species are native to the Great Lakes—American brook, chestnut, silver, and northern brook. Two of them, the chestnut lamprey and the silver lamprey, are parasitic, but any fish attacked by either of those two species is likely to survive. A fish attacked by a sea lamprey, however, is not likely to be so lucky.

According to the US Geological Survey, any fish attacked by a sea lamprey usually dies, either directly from the loss of fluids and tissues or indirectly from a secondary infection.[3] An adult sea lamprey can kill as much as forty pounds of fish in a single year, and in the 1950s, sea lampreys were so dominant that there could have been as many as two million in the Great Lakes during their peak. It's believed that their population declined in Lake Erie only because they ran out of food. With so few fish available, sea lampreys were latching onto anything they could find, including the occasional human out for a summer swim. (Sea lamprey attacks on humans are rare since the organism is evolved to attack cold-blooded animals. Luckily, any human attacked is equipped with the ultimate weapon against the sea lamprey: an opposable thumb that makes it easy to pluck the lamprey off without damage—except to our psyche.)

In 1955, with the commercial fishing industry in a death spiral, the federal governments in the United States and Canada ratified a convention that, among other things, formed the Great Lakes Fishery Commission (GLFC) and set the stage and the tone for six decades of cross-border cooperation.

The GLFC is a binational body charged with finding ways to coordinate research on the Great Lakes and recommend measures to maximize sustained productivity of fish stocks. With governments now coordinating through the fisheries commission, biologists threw themselves into the work of saving the Great Lakes' top predators. "The mind-set was desperation," says Marc Gaden, the communications director and legislative liaison for the GLFC. "There's no other word for it."

Biologists immediately set out to learn everything they could about the life cycle of the sea lamprey—how it spawns, where larvae go after they hatch, what larvae eat, and how they develop into adults. Once biologists understood the life cycle, they could begin to search for a weakness they could exploit.

While researchers were looking for answers, desperate fisheries managers were employing unusual strategies in rivers where the sea lampreys were known to spawn. To block sea lampreys from entering spawning rivers, biologists erected electrical barriers that were only slightly more sophisticated than a plugged-in toaster thrown into a bathtub. Meanwhile, other biologists experimented with building sieve-like structures across rivers to prevent young adult lampreys from swimming out into the lake in search of prey. The problem with that strategy is that the sieves often clogged with sticks and leaves and other debris, blocking the water's normal flow and causing the streams to flood their banks, giving the lamprey a way to get around the barriers.

In 1952, a team of biologists at the Hammond Bay Biological Station in northeastern Michigan was given the job of finding a chemical control

Jugs of the chemical 3 Trifluromethyl-4 Nitrophenol, better known as TFM, are lined up in preparation to be mixed into the Betsie River in northern Lower Michigan. The chemical is applied regularly to Great Lakes tributaries to kill young sea lampreys before they can mature into adults and enter the lake in search of fish.

method for the sea lamprey. The team, led by Vernon Applegate of the US Bureau of Commercial Fisheries, put lampreys and lake trout into large tanks and applied chemicals. If the chemical killed lampreys and didn't kill trout, they would have a solution.

The team screened six thousand compounds, and in 1958, they discovered one that was effective: TFM—3 Trifluromethyl-4 Nitrophenol. The chemical worked on the sea lamprey because, as a primitive organism, it didn't have enzymes in its digestive system that could break down the chemical. Specifically, once the chemical entered the lamprey's bloodstream, it stopped its ability to take in oxygen, essentially suffocating it.

"TFM has been touted as the most important discovery for the Great Lakes ever," says Nick Johnson of the US Geological Survey. "If we didn't have that compound, the fisheries would have collapsed."

The US Fish and Wildlife Service (FWS) and the Fisheries and Oceans Canada (DFO) began to use TFM almost immediately on some 250 rivers in the Great Lakes basin to control the sea lamprey population.

On a chilly, cloudless mid-June morning southeast of Benzie, Michigan, the sea lamprey control team from FWS's Ludington Biological Station is preparing to apply TFM to the Betsie River.

Although today is application day, the team has actually been on site for a couple of days prior to measure the flow and pH of the river. To measure the flow, team members put a red dye in the water and then time how long it takes to get to a certain distance downstream. They do this over a period of several days so they know exactly how much TFM to apply to keep concentrations high enough to kill sea lampreys but low enough not to kill other fish. It's also important to understand the pH of the river because the acidity of the water has an impact on the effectiveness of the lampricide. Sunshine throughout the day increases a river's pH, but it also has the effect of making the lampricide less toxic. Once flow rates and pH are established, it's easy to calculate how much chemical needs to be pumped into the river on an hourly basis over the course of a day. The application, however, walks a fine line: too little and the sea lamprey will survive, too much and other river-dwelling animals will be killed.

On this particular morning, team members have been on the job since seven a.m., running hoses and making sure pumps are working before starting the flow of TFM into the river.

Workers wear protective gear—rubber gloves, rubber aprons, and hip waders—to ensure they don't come in contact with the chemical contained in large jugs labeled both "TOXIC" and "FLAMMABLE." Nearby are two trailers; one hauls the chemicals, and another hauls the equipment. It's still quiet as the team goes to work. The dominant sounds are pumps and an electrical generator. The mechanical drone is broken by calls from red-winged blackbirds, mourning doves, and yellow warblers and the quiet chitchat of the workers. As the team works, it gets assistance from an unexpected helper: an adult bald eagle flies overhead, carrying a squiggling adult sea lamprey in its talons. There's a moment of joy as the eagle flies overhead, but after the eagle disappears, it's back to work.

The team sets the flow rate for 6,800 milliliters a minute and starts to empty the individual jugs into a tub. A hose suctions the poison out of the tub down the embankment to a pump in the river, where it is mixed with water and then pumped into a perforated hose that is stretched across the river and anchored on the opposite bank. A stream of liquid flows out of the hose every eighteen inches, and the toxin is so thoroughly mixed by the time it flows over the dam that the river is now the color of Mountain Dew or lemon-lime Gatorade.

The team checks the flow level every half hour to ensure the proper concentration of poison in the river and make adjustments if necessary. Toxicity needs to be maintained for nine hours for the treatment to be effective. It's a tough juggling act, however, because the pH level decreases as the sun begins to set, and it's important that the river hasn't been made too toxic during the course of the day.

Employees of the US Fish and Wildlife Service applying TFM to the Betsie River in northern Lower Michigan. The chemical is pumped from the holding tank and mixed with river water before being applied to the river. It's critically important to make sure the level of TFM is adjusted throughout the day to ensure the toxin is strong enough to kill young sea lampreys but stays weak enough to prevent the deaths of fish and amphibians that live in the river.

The job of monitoring the concentration downstream goes to Rebecca Neeley, a fish biologist with FWS. Every hour during the course of the day, she draws a small amount of water downstream of the dam and takes it back to her mobile laboratory for analysis. Once she determines the concentration, she will tell the team above the dam whether it needs to increase or decrease the application rate.

On one of Neeley's trips to her laboratory, she learns that one of her coworkers has left her a present—an adult sea lamprey in a tray on a countertop in the lab. Most people wouldn't regard a sea lamprey as a present, but Neeley is thrilled. She quickly identifies this individual as an older adult that has come up the river to spawn and die. She knows this because the lamprey is missing a tooth. Like many older humans, Neeley says, sea lampreys lose their teeth as they age. Neeley likes taking lampreys of this age into classrooms to educate kids about the sea lamprey's impact on the Great Lakes. She says that sometimes the lamprey's teeth fall out in the hands of the children as they are handling them, much to their delight.

———

If the sea lamprey had an ideal spawning ground, the Betsie River just might be it. The river's bottom is sandy in stretches and gravelly in others. The river has a steady flow as it makes its way eleven and a half miles

An adult sea lamprey in an examination tray. The sea lamprey was taken out of the Betsie River in northern Lower Michigan after it had come up the river to spawn and die.

from the Homestead Dam to Lake Betsie and eventually to Lake Michigan. Along the way, there are lots of sandbars, calm backwaters, and quiet tributaries that are perfect for the lamprey's needs. "Every nook and cranny has lamprey in it," Neeley says.

To reproduce, the male will make a depression in the sand or gravel up to three feet wide and six inches deep. If there's a rock in the way, he will grip it with his mouth and move it. In the process of building his nest, he releases a pheromone to attract females. The female will deposit as many as eighty thousand eggs in the depression, which are then fertilized by the male. The adults die shortly after spawning.

Once the young hatch and leave the nest, they are in the larval stage. They will move around the river until they embed themselves in the sandy bottom and let the flow of water bring them food. This is also the life stage when they are most vulnerable to TFM. And while they're in their larval stage, they're also in rivers in large concentrations, which makes control easier; once they become adults, the population spreads out across a huge lake.

The lampreys will stay in the river for three or four years until they develop into adults—which is when they grow their eyes and teeth and swim into the lake like an aquatic vampire seeking blood. After a year in the open water, they swim back up a river to spawn and die. The toxin applied to kill the larvae is ineffective against the eggs, so any lampreys that have been successful in spawning prior to the TFM application will see their offspring survive. That also means that the team will have to return to this location in three or four years for another application.

When the treatment is complete, FWS employees survey the river for evidence that the toxin has killed other fish species. Despite the precautions, TFM applications are an imprecise science, and unexpected large-scale fish kill happens once every two hundred treatments or so, according to Paul Sullivan, the division manager of the Sea Lamprey Control Centre in Sault Ste. Marie, Ontario. "Those kinds of significant kills don't happen very often," Sullivan says. "If it did, we'd be out of business."

Luckily, with the early results coming in, it appears today will be a success. Just a few hours after the application entered the river, Neeley starts to see the result of their efforts—dead sea lamprey larvae washed up on the shore, floating downstream, or being eaten by other animals. The team is actually excited about the dead larvae being eaten by other animals because they say that the TFM will have no impact on them.

One group upset by the regular TFM applications is the Little River Band of Ottawa Indians in Manistee, Michigan. The TFM treatments appear to be undermining their efforts to reestablish lake sturgeon populations. Marty Holtgren, a fish biologist with the Little River Band, says that young lake sturgeon

Rebecca Neeley, a fish biologist with the US Fish and Wildlife Service, examines a young sea lamprey that has been forced to the surface of the Betsie River by an application of TFM.

spend their first summer in many of the same rivers with sea lampreys. The problem is that two western Michigan rivers, the Manistee and Muskegon Rivers, are more alkaline than other rivers in the basin, which makes TFM applications in those two rivers much more toxic than in other Great Lakes tributaries.

The lake sturgeon is considered sacred to many Native Americans in the Great Lakes basin. Austen Brauker, a tribal peacemaker with the Little River Band, says that for him, fishing for sturgeon is a spiritual experience. Before fishing, he places tobacco on the water as a way of asking the fish to come to him and to say thanks for the life he is about to take. If he spears a large fish, he will share it with the tribal community because the act of eating the sturgeon allows him and the other members of the tribe to reconnect with an old friend. "I take it around and give it to people, which is what I do when I catch a steelhead or a deer," Brauker says. "We are communicating again. Our sturgeons are entering our bodies, making our blood and flesh. We share it as feast, and everybody becomes stronger."

FWS has acknowledged the concern over lake sturgeon and in 2014 shifted its TFM treatment on the Muskegon River until mid-September in hopes that the young fish will either have migrated into the lake or will be old enough to withstand the toxin. Moving the treatment to September did not seem to make a difference, however; more than thirty dead young sturgeon were found following the treatment.

Nobody knows exactly how many young lake sturgeon are in the Manistee or Muskegon Rivers at any one time, so it's impossible to know what percentage of sturgeon die with each treatment. Nevertheless, Holtgren does not want to sugarcoat the issue. "Over the past thirty years, there have been significant sturgeon kills" because of TFM, Holtgren says. "We want to see sea lamprey suppressed, but not at the expense of the sturgeon."

———

Now that the toxin has been in the river for a couple of hours, two more FWS employees arrive and prepare to do battle on a second front. These two technicians traveled the river on kayaks earlier in the week and recorded all the potential spots—backwaters, tributaries, and seeps—where a sea lamprey could seek refuge from the chemical. So as morning approaches afternoon, the two again set out in kayaks, this time packing bars of TFM that look like flat pound cakes. Those bars are dropped in areas outside the main flow of the stream and will break down over nine hours, killing any larvae hiding out in these areas. Adding the chemical to the tributaries keeps the concentration in the main waterway high enough to ensure that it's toxic. If the tributaries and seeps are left untreated, eventually they add enough freshwater to the river to render the toxin ineffective downstream. Given the conditions, today the team will apply 319 jugs of TFM, containing 4.8 gallons each in a process that will take about sixteen hours.

––––––––

The team will treat more than twenty rivers this year, traveling as far as upstate New York. Two other FWS teams based in Marquette, Michigan, will cover the west side of Lake Michigan and Lake Superior. The Canadian government bases a similar team in Sault Ste. Marie, Ontario, to treat Canadian rivers and some in upstate New York.

TFM treatments have been so successful that it is estimated that the sea lamprey population in the Great Lakes has been reduced by 90 percent since the 1950s. Sea lamprey control specialists know that despite their successes, they cannot eradicate the sea lamprey. So they've set a more modest goal: maintain its numbers at the current level.

Recently, however, the battle has shifted back in favor of the lamprey. Populations are on the upswing in both Lake Huron and Lake Erie. Toward the end of the first decade of twenty-first century, biologists fanned out to check tributaries for new lamprey breeding areas or to see whether the treatments were somehow becoming less effective. Once the biologists ruled out tributaries as the source of this population increase, they realized that there were only two places the sea lamprey could be coming from: the St. Marys River, which connects Lake Superior and Lake Huron, and the St. Clair River, which connects Lake Huron with Lake St. Clair. That's particularly bad news, according to Paul Sullivan of the Canadian Sea Lamprey Control Center, because no one has the technology to apply TFM to control larvae dug into the gravel bottom of the St. Clair River, which is seventy feet deep in spots and discharges 120 billion gallons of water a day.[4]

In the spring of 2014, both the FWS and DFO surveyed the St. Clair River for areas where larvae are concentrated and discovered the larvae were not in the main channel but in shallower areas in the river delta—places with much slower current. The main channel has good substrate for spawning, but the delta has the sandy bottom that larvae prefer.

Crews from the two agencies made the discovery after they treated areas with Bayluscide, a granular toxin that sinks to the bottom of the river and dissolves in ten minutes. The toxin irritates the lamprey larvae, forcing them to leave the safety of the gravel and swim to the surface. An area is monitored for an hour after it's treated, and crews count and remove larvae in order to determine which areas of the riverbed are most highly populated and will require future treatment.

Although the Bayluscide treatment on the St. Clair River appears to be successful, there's new reason for concern about the possibility of the sea lamprey continuing to spread. According to Nick Johnson, in many cases, an organism can develop a resistance to a treatment within twenty years—similar to the way a bacterium can develop a resistance to antibiotics. Now that TFM has been in use for fifty years, there's good reason to think that it's time to develop new control options.

Starting in 1991, researchers experimented with chemical sterilization of male sea lampreys, but that effort was suspended in 2011 because of the high cost of the program, human health hazards from the chemical, and the difficulty of capturing male sea lampreys prior to breeding.

More recently, researchers at Michigan State University have been looking at using the sea lampreys' own pheromones against them. The goal is to use male sea lamprey pheromones—chemicals produced by an animal to attract a mate—to entice females into an area where they could be trapped and removed before they are able to breed or to lure the females into a river that is unsuitable for larvae development.

In 2004, researchers in the United States, Canada, Japan, Germany, the United Kingdom, and China began to decode the genetic sequence of sea lampreys, which made it possible for the first time to look at unique genes or gene sequences that could lead to new control methods.[5] As a result of that research, biologists in Manitoba and Oklahoma have been looking into ways to interfere with a male sea lamprey's RNA—the nucleic acids that control cell function—to prevent it from being able to reproduce.[6]

––––––––

The sea lamprey is the only example of successful *intentional* invasive-species control in the Great Lakes, and it was only successful because biologists found a weakness they could exploit in the lamprey's life cycle. The alewife population, on the other hand, was controlled by accident.

Growing only about seven inches long, the alewife is a relatively small member of the herring family. Perhaps the most interesting thing about this otherwise unremarkable fish is its many names. In the Canadian Maritimes, it's called the gaspereau. In other parts of its range, it's called the kyak, the sawbelly (because the serrated pattern of its scales on the midline of its belly resemble the teeth of a handsaw), the branch herring, the freshwater herring, and the grayback. Mostly, however, it's known as the alewife. The *Oxford English Dictionary* says the fish may have been given its name because it resembles "a corpulent tavern wife." The *Merriam-Webster Dictionary*, however, says its name may derive from the obsolete word *allowes*, which was once used as an alternate name for shad. Whatever the fish is called, in the Great Lakes, its name became synonymous with environmental disaster.

Alewives were known to be present in Lake Ontario as early as 1873 and may possibly have been native to that lake. Like the sea lamprey, alewives found their way past Niagara Falls through the Welland Canal and were first found in Lake Erie in 1931. Within twenty years, they had expanded into Lakes Huron and Michigan.

Alewives were unable to dominate in Lake Erie because it was too shallow and warm, and they also did poorly in Lake Superior because the water was too cold and remnant lake trout kept their population in check. But Lakes Michigan and Huron were what biologists call "Goldilocks lakes" because, for the alewives at least, they were just right.

In the 1960s, it was estimated that alewives constituted as much as 90 percent of the biomass in Lakes Huron and Michigan.[7] In Lake Michigan alone, it's estimated that there were 167 billion alewives.[8] They were also a stinky, gross nuisance, as millions would die and wash onto beaches in regular events. In fact, so many alewives died in a 1967 episode that it left a one-foot-high pile of carcasses that stretched for three hundred miles on the Lake Michigan shoreline.[9] There were so many fish on Chicago's south side that they had to be disposed of in two Indiana landfills that were specially designated to handle the rotting fish. So many dead alewives blocked the city's water-intake pipes that residents on Chicago's north side were forced to boil their drinking water for months.

With so many alewives in the lake and commercial fishermen looking for something to catch, common sense would suggest that these fish would be somehow economically exploitable, especially since their ocean-based cousins are an important part of the fishing economy of the Canadian Maritime provinces. But Great Lakes alewives are smaller and bonier than their ocean-going cousins, which make them poor quality even for cat food.

With the top predators in the lakes wiped out by sea lamprey, alewife numbers grew unchecked. Alewives not only took control of the food web; they consumed much of the large-bodied plankton in the lake, causing a significant shift in the food web to smaller plankton. The alewives also preyed on young lake trout that previously had been immune from consumption by native fishes. Making matters worse for the lake trout, alewives contain the enzyme thiaminase, which destroys thiamine—vitamin B1—in the predatory fish that consume them. The reduction in thiamine in the adult lake trout resulted in offspring hatching with a birth defect that caused them to swim in a spiral pattern. Eventually, the lack of vitamin B1 caused lethargy and an early death. The lack of vitamin B1 was evident even in fish from wild eggs raised in captivity.

With some species of native fish on the edge of being eliminated from their native ranges and others disappearing from the Great Lakes altogether, fisheries managers saw an opportunity. The decision was made to introduce nonnative salmon from the Pacific Ocean into the Great Lakes.

Salmon were not entirely alien to the Great Lakes, as Atlantic salmon once lived in Lake Ontario before being overfished to extinction, but this would be a massive program of biomanipulation that would change the Great Lakes forever. And it was done for one specific reason: so people would have something—anything—to catch.

———

In September 1964, the state of Michigan hired Howard Tanner as chief of fisheries and gave him one charge: "Do something spectacular." Before coming home to Michigan, Tanner was chief of fisheries research for the state of Colorado. While on fishing trips in the West, he gained experience with coho salmon in freshwater environments and developed an appreciation for the way western states operated with looser bureaucratic rules. When Tanner took over in Michigan, he decided that it was time for change.

Prior to Tanner's arrival, Michigan only managed fish on inland lakes and rivers; Tanner decided it was time to start managing the Great Lakes with the goal of creating the world's best freshwater fishery. Second, he decided the state would manage for sport fishing, not commercial fishing. With the commercial fishing industry being blamed for the collapse of the fish populations in the Great Lakes, the industry did not have many friends in the state legislature. At the same time, people in the middle class had more leisure time to hunt and fish, so why not open fishing up to them as a form of recreation? Once Tanner had established the department's new priorities, he asked fisheries managers in Oregon and Washington if he could have any surplus coho salmon eggs from their hatcheries.

Over the objections of the US Bureau of Commercial Fisheries, Tanner began to stock the lakes with coho salmon. He chose coho because, in those days, lake trout were caught in a fairly boring manner from trolling boats with long lines held down by metal weights. If Tanner was going to get away with introducing nonnatives, he needed to stock fish that would provide "a truly exciting" experience—a fish that would put up a fight and make the angler use both guile and skill to reel it in. In Tanner's mind, the coho salmon was perfect.

In April 1966, the state of Michigan released more than 658,000 year-and-a-half-old salmon into two tributaries of Lake Michigan. With millions of alewives to eat, the fish grew rapidly, and in the late summer and early fall of 1967, the fish came back into those two tributaries to spawn—weighing as much as thirty pounds each. And the rush to catch them was on.

People came from all over the Midwest to fish Lake Michigan. In fact, there were so many people that bait stores ran out of lures, service stations ran out of gasoline, and grocery stores ran out of beer. People lined up elbow to elbow on the inland rivers, and there were so many small boats on Lake

Michigan's Platte Bay north of Frankfort that people onshore swore that you could have walked across the bay on them. The introduction of the coho in Lake Michigan was considered a great success, and it led the state to introduce chinook salmon to the lake a few years later.

Biologists quickly discovered that, like the trout, the salmon could not successfully breed in the wild because they, too, were affected by thiaminase. Once biologists discovered the cause of the vitamin deficiency and added thiamine to fish food in the hatchery, healthy trout and salmon were raised and stocked into the lakes. With the scales tipped back in favor of the predators, the alewives' days were numbered.

So now that the alewife population is a fraction of what it once was, some in the charter fishing industry are worried. Salmon are way down in both size and numbers. One survey found that the chinook salmon population in Lake Michigan fell from 8.4 million in 2012 to just 4.2 million in 2014. That population collapse has some charter captains believing governments should be working to restore the alewife population or believing a rumor that the state of Michigan would soon stock the lake with alewives.

That idea, however, generates an audible guffaw from Ed Eisch, the manager of Michigan's Platte River State Fish Hatchery near Honor, Michigan. Not only is there absolutely no truth to the rumor that the state will stock alewives, but Eisch says he could turn over every single hatchery in the state to alewife production and it would only be enough to feed the predators in the lake for about three days.

Think about that for a second. Only a few decades earlier, alewives were hated because they limited society's use of Lake Michigan for pleasure, and governments were forced to spend money to clean up the beaches of tons of smelly, rotting dead fish. And now people are asking the government to intervene to bring them back?

The collapse of the alewife is a major contributor to what is considered to be the new normal in Lake Michigan and many other parts of the Great Lakes: there's not enough for the top predators to eat. Biologists refer to the constriction of the food web in the middle as a "wasp-waisted" ecosystem, in honor of nineteenth-century corsets women wore to make their waists appear very small. When the ecosystem becomes constricted in the middle like this, it means only bad news for the predators at the top.

And that makes the job of stocking the lakes by state fish hatcheries more difficult. One option is to rebuild the feeder-fish population, potentially with ciscoes, says James Johnson, a research biologist and the manager of the Michigan Department of Natural Resources' Alpena Fishery Research Station. Johnson says his job isn't to fix the lake, because that would be impossible. Instead, he tries to make stocking decisions that adapt to conditions. So, with the amount of plankton in the lake only a fraction of what it once was, Johnson believes ciscoes would be a superior stocking choice as a feeder fish because they have a better chance of surviving in the food-poor conditions than alewives do.

Johnson says that in 1992, the GLFC issued a report that set written population goals for Lake Huron's fish communities on the basis of the amount of fish harvested from the lake in the 1920s. On the basis of those goals, the walleye population is fully recovered, and lake trout is recovering but still a long way from 1920s yields. At a lower trophic level, there are tremendous numbers of chubs in the lake, but because the plankton they eat is so scarce, the chubs no longer grow large enough to harvest. Whitefish, however, have taken the biggest hit. Their population has fallen below what it was when the population report was issued in 1992, and the trajectory is downward. "Whitefish are in a state of decline, and there is no end point," Johnson says. "There's no reason to think we can achieve the lower-trophic-level goals."

The lack of whitefish means there's a big hole in the middle of the food web, and the consequence is that the large predators are feeding on what few fish are in the middle, which helps to prevent the whitefish population from recovering.

Native fish populations could be given an immediate boost, Johnson says, if the other states and the province of Ontario were to remove some of the impoundments and dams in their Great Lakes tributaries. Removing these blockages would allow certain species of fish to return to inland areas where they used to spawn. But, Johnson acknowledges, if those blockages are removed, it would also allow sea lampreys access to vast new stretches of river, making it more difficult and more expensive to control them.

Johnson thinks that it may be time to tell the federal governments that this is their responsibility. "You opened the lakes to these problems, you should be taking care of it," Johnson says. "Don't use the dams as a crutch in lamprey control. If you removed some of these dams, you might be able to close some of Michigan's fish hatcheries."

––––––

The impact of the sea lamprey and the alewife knocked the ecological balance of the Great Lakes out of kilter, and they have yet to recover from that one-two punch. But the experience demonstrated that it is possible to control invasives—at a hefty price. And, unfortunately, as the alewife demonstrates, controlling invasives may also require trade-offs.

Now, another invasive fish, the round goby, is wreaking havoc in the Great Lakes and is raising a new question: is it possible that an invasive organism could become so important to the Great Lakes that attempting to control it would make things worse?

# 3

# LITTLE FISH, BIG TROUBLE

David Jude was counting fish on a contract for Detroit Edison at a power plant on the St. Clair River south of Port Huron, Michigan, in April 1990, when he picked up an unusual specimen. The fish looked like something he had studied many years earlier when he was an undergraduate at the University of Minnesota. The fish was unlike anything he had seen in the Great Lakes because it had a fused pelvic fin.

Jude immediately knew it was a member of the goby family. "What the heck?" he thought.

Jude, who is a now-retired research scientist at the University of Michigan, took the fish to one of his colleagues, Gerry Smith, an expert on fish bones and taxonomy at the University of Michigan Museum of Natural History. Smith took one look and identified the fish as a tubenose goby (*Proterorhinus marmoratus*).

Jude recounted the story of finding the fish to Smith but then figured it was a novelty. "I didn't think it would amount to a hill of beans," Jude says.

Two months later, Jude got a call from a man on the Canadian side of the St. Clair River, not far from where he had been counting fish. The man told Jude that his daughter had caught a goby while she was fishing in the river. Jude was skeptical, but he decided to err on the side of caution and drive to Canada. When Jude arrived at the house, the homeowner told him the fish was downstairs in an aquarium and to go down and have a look. When Jude got to the basement, he was dumbstruck. "I'll be darned," Jude remembers saying. "It's another goby."

Only this was a round goby (*Neogobius melanostomus*). Two individuals of different goby species in the same place meant there was likely an ecological invasion under way, and after thirty years of ecological damage to the Great

33

Lakes caused by the sea lamprey and the alewife, Jude knew this small fish was big trouble for an ecosystem that was just starting to regain its balance.

Jude immediately started asking questions. How did they get into the St. Clair River? Have they become established? How far have they spread? Most importantly, what will the impact be? He discovered soon afterward that gobies were being found in several locations in each of the Great Lakes. Jude quickly realized that all the locations where the gobies were being found had something in common: they were all shipping ports.

Jude guessed the fish were being transported in the ballast water of freighters, but that didn't make sense for one important reason: the round goby does not have a swim bladder, the organ that allows a fish to change depth, and therefore it is restricted to the floor of any body of water it's in. So, if the goby is confined to the bottom, and the ship's ballast intake is just below the surface, how are the fish getting across that gap?

Jude began to figure it out one night when he was sampling larval fish as part of a walleye study in the Muskegon River in western Michigan. Jude and his research team caught round goby larvae in surface-towed nets at night in a river that's thirty feet deep. Jude immediately tried to publish this observation in a scientific journal, but the article was rejected because it lacked daytime data. So Jude and his team went to Ohio State University's Stone Laboratory on Gibraltar Island in Lake Erie to sample for round goby larvae four times during a twenty-four-hour period—day, night, dusk, and dawn. The team caught 167 round goby larvae at night and none during the day.

It was then that Jude realized that round gobies don't need a swim bladder because the larvae are full of lipids and are naturally buoyant and swim up off the bottom at night. Which is exactly how the round goby got into the ballast water: the larvae were sucked into the ballast tanks of a saltwater freighter *at night* as they swam up off the bottom!

On one of those trips home from the St. Clair River, Jude realized just how tough and durable the round goby is. As he was leaving, Jude put a couple of round gobies in a plastic bag without water for his trip back to Ann Arbor. He was stunned to learn upon his arrival in Ann Arbor ninety minutes later that the gobies were still alive. If these fish could survive a ninety-minute trip out of water, they were easily tough enough to survive a several-day journey in the dark of a ballast tank.

Once back in the lab, one of Jude's colleagues, John Janssen, a professor of freshwater sciences at the University of Wisconsin–Milwaukee, decided to replicate the complete darkness of a ballast tank to learn how gobies could find food during a several-day journey. Janssen discovered that gobies did not need light to find food; they could detect vibrations made by potential prey. With this ability, the two scientists realized, the goby would have a tremendous advantage over madtoms, logperch, rainbow darters, and any other native fish that it might compete with for food, giving it the ability to expand rapidly.

The goby's high fecundity and ability to eat invasive zebra and quagga mussels combine to give it a high population density, which helps the goby drive away other species that are competing for spawning space. Even the juvenile gobies have an advantage, as they are able to outcompete native juvenile fish for insect larvae. Finally, the juvenile larvae are also more aggressive and will often grow faster than competing native species.

Like many other invasive species, the round goby spread rapidly, reaching Lake Erie in 1993, southern Lake Michigan in 1994, and Lake Superior in 1995. Everywhere it went, the round goby had a negative impact on native fish, particularly on sculpins, madtoms, bullheads, and darters. In Lake Erie alone, there are an estimated nine billion gobies. "It's bad news for the good guys," Jude says. "It's pretty much an across-the-board decline."

But perhaps the fish that suffered the most from the introduction of the round goby was the mottled sculpin. The goby and sculpin are similar in size and occupy the same niche in the ecosystem. During a study in Calumet Harbor in Lake Michigan, Jude and Janssen documented the more aggressive gobies forcing the sculpins out of prime spawning sites. The gobies arrived in the harbor in 1994, and by 1998, a once healthy sculpin population was all but gone.

––––––

The stories of the round goby and several other particularly insidious invasive species in the Great Lakes are tied closely to ballast water. It appears that the goby, the quagga and the zebra mussel, the spiny water flea, and other exotic species arrived in North America as a result of an act of goodwill. In the mid-1980s, with Russian agriculture struggling and US farmers producing more product than could be consumed domestically, the Reagan administration decided to sell massive amounts of grain to the Soviet Union at subsidized prices. Shortly after that announcement, an armada of rustbucket freighters from the Black and Caspian Seas sailed into Great Lakes ports to pick up the precious food.

The ships may have been taking only grain back across the Atlantic Ocean, but while they were in the Great Lakes, they left something behind: tons and tons of ballast water that originated in eastern European ports.

The act of taking on and discharging ballast water is routine in the shipping industry. Ships usually pump ballast water on board as they unload cargo. That water replaces the weight of the offloaded cargo and gives the ship stability on its journey to its next destination. Once in a new port, the ship will either discharge ballast water as it takes on cargo or take on ballast water as it unloads additional cargo.

In the case of the grain sales, all those Russian ships entering the Great Lakes to pick up cargo dumped their ballast water—and organisms—in unsuspecting ports.

The most unfortunate part is, it could have been prevented. It was possible to stop the goby and all those other organisms in advance, and we knew it.

In 1980, Joe Schormann, a senior program engineer for Environment Canada, commissioned a study to examine the contents of ballast tanks from fifty-five ships that entered the Great Lakes from ten different geographic regions between late August and late October 1980. The researchers found fifty-six different nonnative organisms—an average of about seventeen organisms per ship—and the numbers of individuals per species ranged from ten thousand to about eight billion.[1]

Environment Canada shared the report with both the US and Canadian coast guards, and all three agencies promptly put the report on a shelf to gather dust. After all, thousands of ships from around the world had traveled through the Great Lakes since the St. Lawrence Seaway opened in 1959, and nobody had yet heard the term "invasive species." Why should there be a problem all of a sudden?

"After it came out, it was reviewed by a lot of people from both coast guards," Schormann told the *Toronto Star* in 1989 shortly after the discovery of zebra mussels in Lake St. Clair. "The opinion was fifty-fifty whether it was worthwhile to pursue it and do something or do nothing. Much to my regret, the do-nothing vote won the day, and it was shelved."[2]

But a series of events in the late 1980s caught the attention of regulatory agencies and the US Congress and began to change attitudes. First was the explosion of the population of the Eurasian ruffe.

The ruffe (*Gymnocephalus cernua*) was discovered in the St. Louis River near Duluth, Minnesota, in 1986. In just three years, the ruffe population grew so quickly that it was estimated that it constituted 90 percent of all the biomass in Duluth's harbor. Fear quickly spread that this ugly little fish was going to rule the Great Lakes and spread into the Mississippi River through the Chicago River and Chicago Sanitary and Ship Canal. Suddenly invasive species in the Great Lakes became an important issue in the US Congress, and ballast water, the largest path of introduction, was in the bull's-eye.

Working out of the office of US Senator John Glenn (D-OH), Allegra Cangelosi, who was at that time head of the Great Lakes Task Force for the Northeast-Midwest Institute, went to work on legislation that would require ships entering the Great Lakes to exchange their ballast water at least two hundred miles out to sea and report that exchange to the US Coast Guard. Seawater exchange was viewed as the best and least costly option for a short-term fix because a model analysis revealed that pumping saltwater into ballast tanks would be enough to kill more than 99 percent of freshwater organisms in the tanks.[3] The effectiveness of ballast-water exchange is due to osmotic shock. A freshwater or brackish-water organism can only tolerate so much salinity, and most will die if suddenly hit with the salinity of ocean water.

If there had been any hesitation on the part of Congress to require ballast-water exchange, the legislation became a much easier sell when, during the legislative process, zebra mussels clogged the municipal water intake of Monroe, Michigan, shutting off drinking water to twenty-four thousand people and forcing schools and businesses to close for two days. "The zebra mussel and the ruffe were doing our work for us," Cangelosi says.

In 1990, Congress approved the Nonindigenous Aquatic Nuisance Prevention and Control Act (NANPCA), which did two important things:

- It authorized the US Coast Guard to create ballast-water regulations that would prevent the introduction of nonnative species.

- It created a national invasive-species task force to identify priorities and act as a regional coordinating body for all invasive-species activities. The legislation also authorized a subpanel specifically for the Great Lakes.

Congress gave the job to the US Coast Guard because for more than a century it has been highly effective with maritime regulations and compliance. But since the law was passed, the creation of a sound invasive-species policy has been marred by delay, inaction, and indecision as the US Coast Guard, Transport Canada, states, provinces, two federal governments, the International Maritime Organization, and various nongovernmental organizations all tried to tackle the issue with a developing science and technology that had yet to be invented.

The regulation of water discharges began in 1972, when the US Environmental Protection Agency (EPA) was given responsibility for regulating point sources of pollution under the Clean Water Act. Shortly after the bill passed, the agency decided that it would regulate point-source pollution on land but not regulate ballast-water discharge "incidental to the normal operation of a vessel." At the time, the EPA's decision seemed sensible since ballast water was . . . just water. Even if the EPA had issued ballast-water discharge permits, it would have been to control the discharge of chemicals and petroleum products in the ballast discharges since the water in many European ports was highly polluted. In hindsight, it was an opportunity missed that allowed at least one hundred species to be introduced into the Great Lakes.

In 1990, ten years after Schormann's research on ballast water and a year after the discovery of the zebra mussels in Lake St. Clair, the US Coast Guard was given the responsibility for preventing the introduction and spread of aquatic nuisance species into the Great Lakes through the ballast water of vessels. Meanwhile, the EPA was given responsibility for issuing vessel discharge permits under the Clean Water Act, which meant that two different agencies—with two different staffs and two different authorizations—would be given the joint responsibility to regulate the same substance.

In 1989, the Canadian Coast Guard issued guidelines for shippers to exchange ballast water while at sea, but the guidelines were voluntary.

Reacting to Canada's guidelines, the US Coast Guard in 1992 required ballast-water exchange for ships entering the Great Lakes with pumpable ballast water. The regulation did not, however, include ships that declared no ballast water on board (NOBOBs).

David Reid, a retired research scientist from the National Oceanic and Atmospheric Administration's Great Lakes Environmental Research Laboratory in Ann Arbor, Michigan, who is now an adviser to the Saint Lawrence Seaway Development Corporation, said NOBOBs were not consciously excluded by the regulations; they simply fell through the regulatory-language crack. The focus in the early 1990s was on the discharge of ballast water from foreign ports, and NOBOBs were not considered to be carrying ballast water that could be discharged.

The decision not to require ballast-water exchange for NOBOBs was ultimately a bad one, as Reid later discovered, because even though these ships told the Coast Guard they had no ballast water on board, their ballast tanks usually contained residual water, live organisms, and resting eggs. Those organisms and eggs likely would get discharged at some point during the ship's journey in the Great Lakes system because the ships took on and discharged water as they traveled from port to port.

"No consideration was given to the movement and operations of such vessels once inside US ecosystems or the fact that they might take on local water—which was not covered by the regulations—and then discharge it," Reid says. "That activity simply wasn't recognized as an issue until the late 1990s. It was an omission, but not one made consciously or for political purposes."

It took until 2005, but the Coast Guard eventually made ballast-water exchange a "best management practice" for NOBOBs.

Prior to asking NOBOBs to conduct a ballast-water exchange, the Coast Guard announced in 2004 that it was in the process of establishing ballast-water treatment standards and was looking at ballast-water treatment technologies.

In 1996, Congress approved the National Invasive Species Act (NISA). Among the provisions in the NISA was a measure to create a national ballast-management program that required all ships entering US waters to perform a ballast-water exchange. The measure made the guidelines voluntary, but they would become mandatory if ships failed to show adequate voluntary compliance. Not surprisingly, ships did not show adequate voluntary compliance, and in 2004, the Coast Guard made the program mandatory.[4]

The lack of strong leadership from the federal government—especially from the EPA—created a vacuum that states soon stepped in to fill. At the beginning of the twenty-first century, legislatures in Michigan and New York moved to require that all vessels comply with best management practices for ballast water, and the ships would have to file paperwork that proved they were in compliance. In 2005, additional legislation in Michigan established discharge permits for oceangoing vessels. The permit required all oceangoing vessels to treat ballast water with one of four approved methods before any water could be discharged in state waters or to certify no discharge. The 2005 law was immediately challenged by FedNav, a Canadian shipping company, and other Great Lakes shipping interests. The lawsuit argued that the state's authority was precluded by federal law, and therefore Michigan did not have the power to issue the regulations. The state successfully defended the law, with the court ruling, in part, that the state had the authority to protect its territorial waters, its regulation did not violate the commerce clause of the US Constitution, and the state's authority was not preempted by any federal statute.

Ultimately, however, Michigan's two laws have to be considered a failure. Because neighboring states did not approve similar regulations, the legislation essentially had one unintended effect: most international ships will offload in Michigan ports, but they won't pick anything up. Michigan's regulations are in effect only within the state's borders. For the legislation to have had an impact, it needed to be adopted basin-wide since introduced species do not respect borders.

(Not surprisingly, the issue of employment is part of the ballast-water debate. Since Michigan required ballast-water treatment in 2007, there have been several attempts in the legislature to weaken it. A small but vocal group has argued that the international trade that used to come into Michigan's ports is now going to Ohio, Indiana, and Minnesota.)

In 2006, the Canadian Parliament approved the Canada Shipping Act, which required saltwater flushing for NOBOB ships. Looking to unite policy on both sides of the border, the Saint Lawrence Seaway Development Corporation (SLSDC), the federal agency that operates the US side of the St. Lawrence Seaway, decided to get involved. Knowing that Parliament would be acting on NOBOB ships soon, the organization asked the US Coast Guard for permission to issue NOBOB requirements for ships entering the Great Lakes. Expecting to be tossed out of the room for stepping on the Coast Guard's turf, seaway administrators were surprised when the idea received the Coast Guard's blessing. The Coast Guard realized these regulations were necessary and was thrilled that the corporation could issue the regulations in only ninety days, whereas, due to congressional restrictions, it would take the Coast Guard at least three years to do the same thing.

Craig Middlebrook, deputy administrator of the SLSDC, says some people are unhappy that the agency did not issue tighter regulations, but his agency subscribes to the idea that strong enforcement of a less stringent standard is better and more efficient than a more stringent standard that cannot be enforced.

The game changed dramatically in 2006 when a court finally ordered the EPA to begin to regulate ballast-water discharge on ships. Up until this time, the EPA had rejected every petition to regulate shipping, maintaining that the Clean Water Act did not specifically mandate it. Now, the agency would have to issue vessel discharge permits that would put a limit on the discharge of nonindigenous species in ballast water. Even though the EPA appealed that ruling, the agency immediately started working toward enforcing ballast-water discharge that meets a standard of cleanliness set by an International Maritime Organization (IMO) convention in 2004.

Wisconsin and New York soon followed with legislation requiring ballast water to be treated to a standard that was unachievable with any current technology or even any technology that was on the horizon. Wisconsin required a standard that was one hundred times more strict than the IMO's standard, and New York required a standard that was one thousand times more strict. Both states issued the standards because they believed the regulations would drive the development of new ballast-water treatment technology to protect the lakes. Unfortunately, according to other policy makers and scientists, the regulations were worthless because they were unenforceable. Not only was there no technology available to meet New York's standards; there was no way to measure the number of organisms in ballast water to see if the standard was met.

New York's law also divided the states. In 2011, the governors of Indiana, Ohio, and Wisconsin wrote a joint letter to New York governor Andrew Cuomo asking him to delay or not enforce New York's law because the unachievable ballast-water targets would have the effect of halting international shipping on the lakes.[5]

Robert Reichel, an assistant attorney general for the state of Michigan, says that shippers don't want a patchwork of regulations, and the state governments are not advocating that. But states see that federal legislation has established only a floor for ballast-water treatment but not a ceiling. What's missing, he says, is a national standard that protects water quality and pushes the technology to improve.

(The United States has a history of setting standards that forces technology to advance. Government mandates for clean air, clean water, and improved gas mileage in cars have all been set this way, much to the financial pain of utilities, industries, and automakers and their shareholders and customers but to the benefit of society.)

In 2012, the US Coast Guard set standards for the "allowable concentration of living organisms in ships' ballast water discharged in US waters."[6] The rule applies to all foreign ships and North American ships that travel beyond Anticosti Island in the Gulf of St. Lawrence and requires ships to have a Coast Guard–approved ballast-water management system that meets Coast Guard standards. Ships in the Great Lakes fleet that do not go beyond Anticosti Island are exempt from these regulations until ballast-water treatment technology is available and are instead asked to conduct best management practices for ballast-water discharge.

In 2014, the Vessel Incidental Discharge Act was proposed in Congress. That legislation, sponsored by Senator Mark Begich (D-AK), would have required the US Coast Guard, in consultation with the EPA, to establish and implement uniform national standards and requirements governing ballast-water discharges. Although the legislation boasted an impressive bipartisan list of thirty-two cosponsors, the bill died in committee during an election year. The measure likely would have faced considerable opposition, however, because it prevented states from adopting or enforcing their own ballast-water regulations and required existing state programs to be approved by the Coast Guard.

Despite the lack of recent congressional action, there's new optimism that the ballast-water issue will soon be much closer to a resolution because the EPA and the Coast Guard are now working together. If they're not exactly on the same page, at least they are finally reading from the same book.

In 2013, the EPA issued regulations on ballast-water discharge similar to the Coast Guard's 2012 rules. Both agencies are working on the same time line: vessels built prior to 2013 must have ballast-water treatment installed by January 1, 2016. (Ships built after January 1, 2013, have rudimentary ballast-water treatment systems on board that will be grandfathered in.) The availability of that technology, however, is a big question, and it is entirely possible that this regulation could be delayed. With ballast-water treatment technology on the horizon, the US Coast Guard's new regulations ultimately phase out ballast-water exchange requirements. The EPA and Transport Canada, meanwhile, keep the ballast-water exchange requirement. There's another important difference between the two approaches: the US Coast Guard will give ships and shipping companies extensions that will allow them to comply with the new regulations, realizing that the process is going to take a few years. The EPA, meanwhile, has said it will not be allowing extensions.

Dale Bergeron, a maritime extension educator with Minnesota Sea Grant in Duluth, Minnesota, says that when it comes to ballast-water treatment, both the regulators and the shipping industry are dealing with a "wicked problem." The definition of a wicked problem, he says, is something that changes as you try to solve it. For ballast-water regulation, here's the problem: the EPA can regulate water quality on a contingency basis, which means it can change the standards as it sees fit. If the EPA wants to force the ballast-water discharge standards higher, it can do that. It is a system that has worked with both automakers and smokestack polluters like utilities.

One other problem: Bergeron says the US Coast Guard asked shippers to install early ballast-water treatment systems even before it vetted the systems that will eventually be required. The Coast Guard did so knowing it would take a long time to approve the backlog of ballast-water systems—so it encouraged shippers to install ballast-water systems knowing full well that the systems would likely not meet standards. The Coast Guard's firm stand creates a problem for some shipping companies because they own only one or two ships. These companies are so small, Bergeron says, that they cannot afford the expense of installing a $2 million ballast-water treatment system and then discover five years later that system doesn't meet Coast Guard regulations.

Despite the uncertainty, FedNav, the same company that sued the state of Michigan in 2005, announced in 2015 that it would be installing the BallastAce water-treatment system in twelve oceangoing ships under construction in Japan. Even though the treatment system has been approved by the Japanese government, it has not yet received US Coast Guard approval. FedNav likely decided to install the system in these new ships because each would only cost $500,000 to install during construction and would cost considerably more to install on an existing ship. As of 2015, the company owned eighty oceangoing ships; thirty-four of those regularly called on ports in the Great Lakes.

Meanwhile, there's a huge risk for the companies that build ballast-water treatment systems. After working for ten years and spending several million dollars on research and development, any company that did not receive certification for its ballast-water systems after that would likely be forced to go out of business.

The good news, Bergeron says, is that both the shipping and regulatory communities on the federal level understand that there's a conundrum and are trying to deal with it. "We are moving forward, but not at a time line that anybody is happy about," Bergeron says. "Everybody is mad, regulators and shippers."

————

Before any ballast-water treatment system can be installed on a ship, the technology must meet regulations set by the International Maritime Organization's Ballast Water Management Convention in 2004 and be certified by the US Coast Guard. The IMO's treaty has a goal of reducing the spread of ship-borne organisms around the world by setting ballast-water standards for both ballast-water exchange (referred to in the shipping industry as the D1 regulation) and ballast-water treatment (the D2 regulation) that would be phased in over time. Because the vast majority of shipping goes in and out of saltwater ports, the technology vendors are concentrating on creating ballast-water treatment systems for oceangoing ships. That means the Great Lakes may end up being the red-haired stepchild in the development of adequate technology because only a fraction of shipping occurs on freshwater.

Meanwhile, the states and federal agencies have developed the ethic that if it's good enough for the IMO, it should be good enough for the Great Lakes. Unfortunately, the IMO's D2 standard of ten or fewer organisms fifty microns in size in a cubic meter of water is really just a best guess that developed out of a series of meetings and is not based on any science or achievable goals. It's widely agreed that the standards lessen the odds for an invasion, but they fall way short of preventing the additional transfer of organisms around the world. The IMO standards also fail to address viruses and bacteria, which are particular concerns in saltwater ports. Even if the treaty is a step in the right direction, there's no guarantee that it will ever go into effect; it has to be approved by thirty nations whose combined trade represents at least 35 percent of the world's shipping tonnage. (As you can imagine, the ratification of the treaty by the tiny island nation of Kiribati doesn't go very far toward the 35 percent threshold.) Canada ratified the treaty in 2010 but does not enforce it. The United States sent a delegation to the 2004 convention and had considerable input in the development of the standards, but the United States will not ratify the treaty because it does not feel it is rigorous enough. As of July 1, 2015, forty-four nations representing 32.86 percent of the world's shipping tonnage had approved the pact, and several others were said to be on the verge of submitting their notice of ratification.[7]

––––––

The ratification process likely came to a screeching halt on October 5, 2015, when a three-judge panel of the Second Circuit Court of Appeals ruled that the EPA acted arbitrarily when it adopted the IMO's standards, especially since ballast-water treatment technology is available that would allow the EPA to set a more strict standard—perhaps by a factor of ten. The ruling came as a result of a lawsuit filed by four environmental groups that contended that the EPA ignored ballast-water treatment technology and should have adopted standards that are more stringent than the IMO's.

"The EPA appeared to take the path of least resistance by adopting an existing international standard that is inadequate to prevent . . . colonization,"

said Allison LaPlante, a professor at Lewis and Clark Law School in Port-
land, Oregon. LaPlante represented the four groups that brought the lawsuit.

The ruling allows the EPA to continue to issue ballast-water permits
to vessels entering the United States until 2018, when the current permits
expire. The agency will then issue new vessel discharge permits using the
yet-to-be-set standard.

The court's ruling is likely to have an unintended consequence: those
nations that had planned to submit their IMO ballast-water ramification
notice will now likely wait to see what the EPA will do, further delaying
implementation of the IMO's weak standards and facilitating the continued
transfer of organisms by ballast water.

The US and Canadian governments were forced to reconsider their
NOBOB regulations after David Reid of the National Oceanic and Atmospheric Administration and his colleague Hugh MacIsaac began to crawl
around inside the ballast tanks of international freighters in an effort to get
a handle on the problem. MacIsaac, a professor who studies invasion biology at the University of Windsor's Great Lakes Institute for Environmental
Research, started his career studying the impacts of zebra mussels on the
Great Lakes ecosystem but quickly came to realize that unless the focus
shifted to prevention, he would likely be studying the impacts of a new invasive species every year or two.

Reid and MacIsaac devised a plan to look at ballast water on international
ships and quickly realized that even if a ship declared there was no ballast on
board, the ballast tanks still likely contained a small amount of water with
organisms and a layer of sediment in the bottom of the tanks that contained
plankton and fish eggs. By tracking these ships' movements around the lakes,
they discovered that the NOBOBs filled and drained their ballast tanks several times as the ships traveled from port to port. Not only were these ships
leaving water and organisms from Europe in Great Lakes ports; they were
moving organisms around the Great Lakes from port to port.

In 2000, MacIsaac and Reid were approached by the Great Lakes Protection Fund, a Chicago-based private endowment created by Great Lakes
governors, and asked to answer a simple question: how effective is ballast-
water exchange?

The two researchers set up a series of tests on ships leaving for Europe
with water from the Great Lakes in their ballast tanks. On the journey across
the Atlantic Ocean, the ships flushed their ballast tanks with saltwater, and
when the ships reached Europe, MacIsaac and Reid checked for organisms. The two researchers discovered that this simple ballast-water exchange
procedure was 99 percent effective; the exchange reduced the number of

individual organisms to a level where it would make the odds against invasion extremely high.

Biologists are able to estimate the chances of yet another organism becoming invasive through two concepts that are all about mathematics and probability: the Allee effect and propagule pressure. The Allee effect is a concept named after Warder Clyde Allee, a zoologist at the University of Chicago, who noticed that in many species undercrowding was the top factor in limiting population growth.

Propagule pressure is also a key to understanding why some invasions succeed while others fail. Let's say Pitor and Paulina Propagule are living happily in the Caspian Sea. To their surprise, they get pumped into a ship's ballast tank, survive the trip across the Atlantic, and get pumped out into a Great Lakes port. These two individual organisms may live long, happy lives in their new ecosystem, but the odds are slim that they will be able to find each other to reproduce, based on the concept of the Allee effect. Even if they manage to find each other, the odds are still low that they will be able to establish a new population. If a ship pumped one hundred thousand individual Pitors and Paulinas into the same harbor, however, the odds of establishment and invasion increase dramatically, based on the concept of propagule pressure. That concept is a measure of the number of individuals introduced into an area. As the number of releases or the number of individuals increases, the risk of establishment increases. Therefore, any policy that reduces the number of propagules—like saltwater exchange or ballast-water treatment—reduces the probability of establishment.

The efforts of MacIsaac and Reid led to the creation of the Sea Ballast Water Working Group, an organization that is now working to harmonize cross-border ballast-water efforts. That organization is made up of the US Coast Guard, the US Saint Lawrence Seaway Development Corporation, Transport Canada, and the Canadian St. Lawrence Seaway Management Corporation. So far, the organization has focused on an inspection program that appears to be a success. Since 2013, the ballast tanks of every ship entering the Great Lakes were inspected by the US Coast Guard to make sure ballast water in the tanks is at least thirty parts per thousand of salinity. If the ballast-water exchange fails to reach that level of salinity, the ship is required to return to sea for additional ballast-water exchange. The ship's captain has the option to continue on to inland ports if the captain agrees to allow the Coast Guard to seal the tanks for the entire journey. At the end of the journey, the captain must prove to the Coast Guard that the tanks are still sealed. Any violation of that requirement results in a fine of US$36,000 per incident. Aquatic organisms that may have attached to a ship's hull in a previous freshwater port are not a concern, as they are unable to survive the journey in saltwater.

Saltwater exchange has been so effective at reducing propagule pressure that a new ballast-water-introduced species has not been discovered in the Great Lakes since 2006. That little factoid means two things. First, saltwater exchange has been effective at reducing the introduction of exotics in the Great Lakes. Second, the extended period since the last introduction means that we've been lucky. Ballast-water exchange is far from a foolproof method of protection, because Mother Nature has created creatures that can survive the best ballast-water treatment technology that exists today. Mother Nature has also produced organisms that can breed asexually, which means that if just one individual slips through, it's invasion on.

The fear of that one superorganism surviving saltwater exchange is why the state of Michigan moved to require onboard ballast water be treated with one of four approved methods before it can be discharged. Unlike the Coast Guard, the state does not require the discharge to meet a numerical standard.

Now that the Coast Guard has set numerical standards, everybody from mom-and-pop inventors to multinational corporations has developed treatment systems. Before any of those systems can be installed in new ships or retrofitted to existing ships, it needs to be approved to receive certification, which is where the Great Ships Initiative comes in.

In Superior, Wisconsin, on a small spit of land extending out into Duluth-Superior Harbor, the Great Ships Initiative testing lab looks more like a gigantic Tinker Toy setup than a laboratory that is trying to find worldwide solutions. Brightly colored red, yellow, and blue pipes and large white tanks dominate the facility. Despite the almost kindergarten-like look of the facility, companies from all over the world ship their treatment systems here to have both their design and finished models tested. The goal of the ballast-water treatment system is to meet the US Coast Guard regulation of ten or fewer organisms fifty microns in size in a cubic meter of water.

The Great Ships Initiative is a project of the Northeast-Midwest Institute, a Washington, DC–based nonprofit. Superior seems like an unusual place for a DC-based think tank to be operating a research project. It's a long way from big cities and large universities that could provide additional resources. In reality, there's no place better.

The facility is able to take in large amounts of water—and plankton—right from Duluth-Superior Harbor, run it through the treatment system to be tested, and then dispose of the water properly. Ballast-water treatment systems need to be tested on the Great Lakes because the freshwater ecosystem is significantly different from brackish and saltwater ecosystems. In particular, a large proportion of the Great Lakes zooplankton are extremely small plankton and can easily pass through filtration systems designed for saltwater. To ensure that tests are challenging, the facility can add concentrated algae and turbidity to the lake water if its natural levels are too low to perform an adequate test.

Allegra Cangelosi, the same US Senate staffer who started her career fighting the spread of the ruffe in 1986, is now the principal investigator for the Great Ships Initiative. She took on the job because as president of the Northeast-Midwest Institute, she became all too aware that people working on the ballast-water issue had lots of opinions and very little data. So she applied for a series of grants, put together the facility in 2008, and set about to test systems and assumptions.

Since then, she says the facility has been making what she calls "invisible progress." Many of the treatment-system vendors have already gone through one round of testing at the facility and are now using that data to recalibrate and fine-tune their systems to receive US Coast Guard approval for installation and use. In 2015, the facility added equipment that allows it to perform system certification testing on equipment already installed on ships.

———

So, knowing that it is unlikely that the ballast-water issue will be 100 percent solved anytime soon, why not just shut down the St. Lawrence Seaway? What's the problem with having the saltwater freighters drop off and pick up their cargo somewhere near Montreal? Besides, the seaway is functionally obsolete. Most of the world's goods are shipped on huge container ships that are unable to make it into the Great Lakes because the seaway's locks are too small to handle them.

Every now and then, someone whispers this thought and is promptly ignored. The St. Lawrence Seaway, by the estimates of the two corporations that run it, generates $36 billion in economic activity and is responsible for 227,000 jobs in the United States and Canada.

———

Progress has been slow and a long time coming on the ballast-water issue, and in retrospect, it's painfully clear that it would have been far more difficult for exotic species—including the round goby—to enter the Great Lakes ecosystem if the Coast Guard, the EPA, or Transport Canada had realized the potential for the problem and imposed ballast-water exchange regulations in the 1970s.

Nevertheless, the goby is here today—an estimated nine billion of them in Lake Erie alone—and it is decimating the native fish population through its consumption of eggs. David Jude says he has seen videos made by scuba divers of gobies gathered around a bass protecting its eggs in a nest. The video showed the gobies waiting patiently around the bass until one individual goby loses patience and ventures in an attempt to snatch an egg. When the bass reacts and leaves the nest to chase the first goby, the other gobies overrun the nest and devour the eggs. Jude says the minimum impact is increased stress on native fish and decreased survival rates.

Other invasives, like the rusty crayfish, eat fish eggs, but the gobies' sheer numbers make them a bigger threat. The goby's famous appetite was evident during one episode when Department of Natural Resources (DNR) employees attempted to "seed" a Lake Michigan reef by pouring a jar of fertilized trout eggs on it. The goal was to have the trout eggs sink into the nooks and crannies between the rocks so they would be protected from hungry gobies. The project failed, however, because as soon as the containers were opened, the gobies rushed to consume the eggs, and at least one entered the egg container while it was in the diver's hand.

Despite the goby's caviar-like diet, any predator that eats a goby is getting a meal that's only slightly better than junk food. A goby contains about half as much energy as a native Great Lakes fish, so any predator consuming a goby will have to eat twice as much to have the same energy intake. Unfortunately, there's only so much room in a fish's digestive tract.

Upon introduction, the goby spread quickly through the Great Lakes because the native fish either failed to recognize it as prey or couldn't figure out how to eat it. Now, lake trout and smallmouth bass are scooping up gobies like crazy. And that makes Dave Rommel very happy.

Rommel is the owner of Big Bob's Bait and Tackle in Frankfort, Michigan, and through the windows in his store, he can see Betsie Lake sparkling in the distance, across the street and down the hill. From his customers and neighbors and through the media, he's heard the gloom-and-doom talk about what invasive species are going to do to the Great Lakes—and consequently his business—and isn't worried. In fact, Rommel says that the arrival of the round goby has been good for business. Now that lake trout are gorging on gobies, their flesh is less greasy, and the color of their skin has changed from a muddy gray to a darker, richer color with more prominent rings and orange gills. Those changes to the trout's anatomy make it more attractive to catch and eat. "The lake will take care of itself," Rommel says.

James Johnson, manager of the Michigan DNR's Alpena Fishery Research Station, says he reacted with alarm when he saw his first round goby in Lake Huron, but like Rommel, he now knows the situation could be much worse. In the absence of the alewife, the goby has become an important addition to the way energy is transferred in the food web because adult gobies are one of the few fish that can eat invasive zebra and quagga mussels. When the gobies eat the mussels, they not only control the mussel population; they convert nutrients in mussels into something that the big native fish can eat. The gobies are so dependent on the zebra and quagga mussels for food that Jeff Tyson, the Lake Erie fisheries program administrator for the Ohio DNR, believes if something caused the mussels to disappear, the goby population would greatly suffer.

Jude says young gobies eat mostly insect larvae and a few mussels before they develop a shell, while bigger gobies eat more mussels. Even though the gobies consume both juvenile and adult mussels, they don't eat enough to act as a control on the zebra mussel population. In areas with large goby populations, however, it's difficult to find young zebra mussels. Adult gobies, meanwhile, have jaws strong enough to eat the adult mussels, shell and all. Even though the mussel is attached to a rock or some other hard surface, the goby will grab the mussel in its mouth and roll its body to rip the mussel from its base before eating it.

Ellen Marsden, a professor of fisheries at the University of Vermont, has been working with the Michigan DNR to reestablish a lake trout breeding population in Lake Huron's Thunder Bay. That population was wiped out by pollution from a cement plant near Alpena, Michigan, in the 1960s and 1970s. Recently, the Michigan DNR has built twenty-nine new lake trout spawning reefs, and Marsden's job was to monitor the reefs for trout larvae and to ensure zebra and quagga mussels weren't becoming so thick on the reefs that their presence would prevent the trout eggs from settling in the substrate.

During her research, Marsden noticed a change in goby behavior— they're no longer the brazen little thugs they once were. Gobies now hide out for protection because the lake trout learned to eat them, and they have also become a favorite meal of loons, cormorants, and other diving waterbirds. The double-crested cormorant is the bird that anglers love to hate because it's widely believed the bird is responsible for the drop in sport-fish populations in the Great Lakes. The cormorant, however, is one of the anglers' best allies. Regular surveys of the contents of cormorants' stomachs across the Great Lakes basin conducted by state and provincial wildlife managers have showed that the goby is far and away the cormorants' number-one prey item from May through October.

The relationship between the round goby and native predators is just one illustration of how invasive species have become well integrated into the Great Lakes food web. In fact, gobies are credited with preventing the extinction of a subspecies of the northern water snake that makes its home on islands in Ohio waters in the western basin of Lake Erie. As a result of a combination of human persecution and the destruction of habitat on islands that are dense with lake cottages and vacation homes, the Lake Erie water snake's population fell to about two thousand. In 1999, the snake was given

federal protection in both the United States and Canada. Through the combination of the protection and an appetite for the booming goby, the snake's
population improved to twelve thousand by 2008. It was removed from the
endangered species list in the United States in 2011, but it continues to be
listed as threatened in Canada because there is less appropriate habitat.

Kristen Stanford, a herpetologist with Ohio State University's Stone
Laboratory, says the Lake Erie water snake is now almost totally dependent
on round goby for food. Her research team's survey of the snakes' diet in 2013
showed that 98 percent of its food was round goby. Ironically, as part of the
post-delisting monitoring demanded by the US Fish and Wildlife Service,
researchers are now required to monitor the health of near-shore goby populations. That's because if the goby populations were to crash, Stanford says,
it's likely that the water snake's population would suffer as well. The snake
can't go back to its pre-goby diet—bullheads, madtoms, catfish, shiners, and
sculpins—because those species are largely gone from Lake Erie, victims of
competition with the goby.

The relationship between the water snake and the goby is not the only
case that demonstrates how some rare and threatened North American
species have come to rely on invasive species for their continued survival.
In California, Arizona, and Colorado, the southwest willow flycatcher, an
endangered subspecies of the willow flycatcher, now relies heavily on the
tamarisk—a tree native to Africa and Eurasia—for nesting habitat. In the
San Francisco Bay Area, the California clapper rail, an endangered subspecies of the clapper rail, now relies on smooth cordgrass (*Spartina alterniflora*),
a grass native to western Europe and Africa. According to one study, any
effort to remove any of the cordgrass without first creating ample native
habitat would be detrimental to the rail.[8]

---

The goby may have had a hand in reviving the population of the Lake
Erie water snake, but it's clear it has had a devastating impact on Great
Lakes fish. But the goby's rapid expansion across the Great Lakes may be
slowing or starting to decline soon.

The round goby's rapid expansion across the Great Lakes was made possible by the presence of two other invasive organisms—the zebra mussel and
the quagga mussel. The three species lived side by side back in Eurasia, and
the mussels' presence in the Great Lakes made the goby's transition to its
new ecosystem that much easier by providing it with a little home cooking.

But the damage done to the Great Lakes by the zebra and quagga mussels makes the goby look like a mere pest.

# 4

## MUSSEL MUSCLE

The possibilities of a fresh-water shell like the "zebra mussel" being introduced is very great. There is entirely too much reckless dumping of aquaria into our ponds and streams. A number of foreign fresh-water shells, etc., have been introduced in this way. Why not the mussel? This was the way the water-hyacinth was introduced into the St. Johns River, Florida.

Charles W. Johnson, principal curator,
Boston Society of Natural History, 1921

There are about thirty-five people on the glass-bottomed *Lady Michigan* this morning as it pulls away from its dock at the National Oceanic and Atmospheric Administration's Great Lakes Maritime Heritage Center on the Thunder Bay River in Alpena, Michigan. Although most people on board are from the Midwest, some have come from as far away as Arizona to take this shipwreck tour in Lake Huron's Thunder Bay National Marine Sanctuary.

Once on board, the passengers are spread out. Some head for the top deck to enjoy the sun and view, while others settle inside the cabin on the lower deck to be able to claim a spot on the railings that surround the glass panels built into the hull of the boat.

It's a quiet mid-June morning. Men and boys fish along the shoreline where just a month earlier a local fifth-grade class had worked on a project investigating rusty crayfish, an invasive that now dominates the river bottom. There's a layer of pollen on the water and high clouds make for a milky sky, but otherwise it's a perfect day; it's not too hot and not too cold, and most importantly for anybody with a weak stomach, Lake Huron is calm.

The boat slowly makes its way down the river, under the Second Avenue drawbridge, past the marina on the right and the wood products plant on the left. When it reaches the open water of Thunder Bay, it makes a right turn and heads south. The boat first hovers over the wreck of the *Shamrock*, which was sunk here on purpose in the late 1800s. The hull's glass panels magnify everything below it by one and a half times, so it makes a seaweed-covered anchor appear much closer than it really is. After a few minutes, the boat moves on to two other wrecks before heading north to today's featured shipwreck, *Scanlon's Barge*.

The wooden barge sank in twenty feet of water northeast of Alpena, but for some reason, nobody knows exactly when. People gather around the glass panels and marvel at the algae-covered planks, cranes, and winches. Besides the algae, zebra mussels and round gobies have also made this wreck their home. A smallmouth bass is the only native fish that can be seen through the glass panels.

While hovering over the wreck of *Scanlon's Barge*, a woman from Pennsylvania on the upper deck of the boat marvels at her ability to see the wreck in twenty feet of water. "It's amazing how clear it is!" she says.

Yes, it is amazing how clear the water is. And it's a troubling indicator that something critically important is missing from the Great Lakes ecosystem.

———

Twenty-five years ago, it might have been impossible to run a shipwreck tour here. Certainly, it would have been far more difficult for a person to stand on the top deck of the *Lady Michigan* and see the bottom, let alone a shipwreck with clarity. But the shipwreck tours are enhanced today because of the impact of two invasive species, the zebra mussel (*Dreissena polymorpha*) and the quagga mussel (*Dreissena bugensis rostriformis*). Both mussels are closely related members of the dreissenid family and are native to the Dnieper River and Caspian and Black Seas in eastern Europe. The zebra mussel was named for the striped pattern on its shell. The quagga mussel has similar striping on its shell and was named after the quagga, an extinct subspecies of zebra. Neither mussel is particularly large—both only about the size of a pistachio, with the quagga mussel being slightly larger. Both mussels have a similar life span of three to five years. Really, the only major differences are that the quagga mussel can subsist in colder, deeper water where there is less food and it can be perfectly happy living on a sandy lake bottom that would discourage a zebra mussel.

Scientists usually have a difficult time drawing a direct cause-and-effect conclusion on the impact that any one invasive organism is having on the Great Lakes. That is because so many invasives have arrived and there have

Quagga mussel shells on a Lake Erie shoreline. Many biologists believe that of all the nonnative species that are now in the Great Lakes, none has had a larger impact than the quagga mussel.

been so many other dramatic changes in such a short period of time that it's often difficult to tell which organism is responsible for what. In the case of the zebra and quagga mussels, however, the cause and effect is as clear as the water itself. There are so many voracious zebra and quagga mussels eating so much that they have stripped the lakes of much of the phytoplankton—the microscopic plants that are the base of the food web—thus rearranging the flow of energy and nutrients through the food web.

The mussels are filter feeders, which means they suck in food, consuming what they want and spitting out what they don't. Both species are capable of filtering more than a liter of water a day. While a liter may not sound like much, there are so many dreissenid mussels in Lake St. Clair that they have the capacity to filter all the water in the lake in just four days. One study by researchers at Buffalo State University in New York shows that the mussels have had a bigger impact on Lake Erie's benthic community than decades of pollution from the 1940s through the 1970s.[1]

In fact, the dreissenid mussel population has grown so large that it has all but wiped out the annual bloom of diatoms, a type of calorie-rich plankton.

There are about fourteen hundred different species of diatoms in the Great Lakes alone, and about 50 percent of all living things in the world are diatoms. They are—or were—so plentiful that many zooplankton and small fish eat only diatoms. That made the spring diatom bloom critically important to life in the Great Lakes because it had the effect of jump-starting the food web for spring and summer months, providing critical energy and nutrients for larvae and adult fish just as they were coming out of winter torpor.

Prior to the arrival of the mussels, the bloom was so large that it could be seen on satellite images. Today, the spring bloom has been reduced by two-thirds. The only lake that still has a substantial diatom bloom is Lake Superior. Coincidentally, Superior is the lake with the fewest dreissenids.

It may sound like the mussels are causing irreparable harm to the lakes. In some ways, that is true. The mussels are actually changing the chemistry of the water by depositing large amounts of calcium from their deteriorating shells on the benthic layer. The mussels are also removing and redistributing phosphorus. When they eat phytoplankton, the mussels consume and use phosphorus taken in by the phytoplankton. But because the mussels consume more plankton than they need for their own growth and energy purposes, they excrete the excess phosphorus to the lake floor, making it unavailable for new phytoplankton.

Ironically, the mussels are having the effect of reversing two centuries of human impacts on the lakes and are returning water-clarity levels to those that existed prior to European settlement. David Jude, the University of Michigan researcher who discovered the goby in the St. Clair River, says that in terms of plankton abundance, Lake Huron is starting to look more like Lake Superior, and Lake Michigan is not far behind.

Scientists have a pretty good idea of how much plankton was in the lakes three hundred years ago on the basis of sediment core samples taken from lake beds. Those sediment samples show that over the past three centuries, humans have caused phytoplankton to explode (in Lakes Michigan and Erie in particular) through the input of nitrogen and phosphorus from human wastewater and agriculture. Scientists call the process of enriching the lakes *eutrophication*, and the phytoplankton explosion caused by eutrophication did two things. First, it caused the water to become more turbid, which benefited certain fish species like the walleye. Second, an abundance of plankton provided a plentiful food source for small fish, especially the alewife, which in turn provided many small fish for the top predators.

In the 1970s, however, pollution-control efforts began to cut the phosphorus flow into the lakes, which caused a decline in phytoplankton. That, along with the introduction of salmon, spurred the crash of the alewife population.

As the lakes became less productive, this also shifted the advantage back to the native species that can manage nicely in areas with less food.

But it's not just the fish that have been affected by the mussels. The number-one victim of the dreissenid mussels appears to be *Diporeia*, a small, shrimp-like creature that until recently was one of the most common benthic organisms in the lakes' deeper offshore waters. The disappearance of *Diporeia* may be the most important negative change caused by the dreissenid mussels because, unlike some species benefiting from improved water clarity, there's no trade-off here.

Before retiring from the National Oceanic and Atmospheric Administration's Great Lakes Environmental Research Laboratory in Ann Arbor, Michigan, Thomas Nalepa was an aquatic biologist tracking changes in the depths of the Great Lakes and was among the first biologists to research the impacts of the zebra mussels in North America. When Nalepa began his research, one of the most abundant organisms at the benthic layer was *Diporeia*, a glacial relict that does well in cold, deep water and was a critical food for Great Lakes fish because it was abundant, readily available to fish, and high in lipids and therefore high in calories. In samples taken from southern Lake Michigan in the 1980s, *Diporeia* was present in population densities up to twenty thousand individuals per square meter. But in 1992, *Diporeia* began to disappear. Nalepa's spring survey found ten thousand individuals per square meter, which wouldn't necessarily be a reason to panic. But alarm bells started ringing when the summer survey found only five thousand individuals, and the fall survey found none.

Nalepa was shocked. He knew that zebra mussels had arrived in Lake Michigan but hadn't really considered the impact that they would have on *Diporeia* and the food web until that moment. Nalepa was also puzzled. Even though the decline in the *Diporeia* and the arrival of the zebra mussels matched up perfectly, Nalepa could not define a direct cause-and-effect relationship. The zebra mussels and *Diporeia* likely compete directly for food, but even though the *Diporeia* were in decline, there was no indication that they were in trouble. In fact, individual *Diporeia* that were caught in the fall in other, nearby sections of Lake Michigan showed no sign of stress; they were not underweight, infected with parasites, or in any other way obviously weakened.

The mystery was further compounded when others began to look at *Diporeia* populations in other places—specifically at the population in the Finger Lakes in New York—and discovered that the mussels seemed to have no impact on the organism there; that is, *Diporeia* populations remained high despite high numbers of mussels.

Although the reason is unclear, it is established beyond question that the mussels are having a tremendous impact on Great Lakes *Diporeia*. On the basis of lake-wide surveys between the mid-1990s and 2010, the *Diporeia* population in Lake Michigan has declined by 97 percent. That decline has had a dramatic impact on the lake whitefish population, which has also seen its population decline and individual fish become lighter and smaller. That's partially because the whitefish that survive to adulthood are now forced to eat quagga mussels to survive, says Dan O'Keefe, an extension coordinator with Michigan Sea Grant. O'Keefe says after the initial expansion of zebra mussels, the weight of the average whitefish in southern Lake Michigan declined from 5.48 pounds at age seven to 3.93 pounds.

With the phytoplankton greatly reduced, the amount of light that penetrates deep water has increased dramatically. For decades, Gary Fahnenstiel, the now-retired director of the National Oceanic and Atmospheric Administration's Lake Michigan Field Station in Muskegon, Michigan, used Secchi disks—small round disks with alternating black-and-white pie-shaped quadrants—to document changes in water clarity in Lake Michigan. The disks are anchored to a line or mounted to a pole and are submerged. When the researcher can no longer see the submerged disk from the surface, the depth is recorded. For decades, Fahnenstiel had consistently recorded Secchi depths in Lake Michigan at between five and six meters. In 2007, Fahnenstiel realized the impact the quagga mussels specifically were having when suddenly the Secchi depth grew to sixteen meters. And in 2010, he found a location in the lake near Frankfort, Michigan, with a Secchi depth that was at least thirty meters. Fahnenstiel said the real Secchi depth was never determined because he and his research team ran out of line.

———

For some aquatic birds, the increase in water clarity is having deadly consequences. Since the late 1990s, more than one hundred thousand loons, grebes, ducks, cormorants, and gulls have died from the bacterium that causes botulism. *Clostridium botulinum* Type-E occurs naturally in Great Lakes sediments and in soils on land in the spore stage of the bacterium's life cycle. But in the Great Lakes recently, it appears that increased water clarity and hotter summers combined with the presence of two invasives have set off a chain reaction.

In simple terms, here's how biologists describe it: Clearer and warmer water promotes the growth of algae. When those algae die late in the summer, they sink to the bottom and rot in the benthic layer, depleting the water of oxygen. This anaerobic situation—with a combination of the correct water temperature, pH, and lake level—causes the *Clostridium botulinum* spores to germinate. Those spores produce a toxin that paralyzes the central nervous systems of the vertebrates that consume it. It is assumed that waterfowl that consume fish carrying the toxin are quickly affected and lose the ability to use their muscles and become unable to fly or walk on land. Eventually, they lose the ability to control the muscles in their necks and are unable to keep their heads above water and drown.

There have been periodic botulism outbreaks in the Great Lakes since the 1960s, but the number and severity of the outbreaks have grown dramatically since the arrival of the goby. Yes, the mussels are making the water clearer, and algae are now able to grow at deeper depths and in more places, which gives botulism spores more area to grow; but it appears that the gobies are delivering the toxin to the waterbirds.

Jill Leonard, a fish biologist at Northern Michigan University in Marquette, Michigan, says it appears that the bottom-feeding gobies are eating contaminated zebra and quagga mussels and then transferring the toxin to the birds. As of right now, however, there's no way to know for certain. Researchers know that botulism is killing the birds because they can detect the toxin in the birds' blood. They also know that the birds are eating the gobies because they are finding goby bones in the birds' stomachs. The problem is, in the time between eating the contaminated fish and death, the bird will have digested and excreted any fish that may have been carrying the botulism. If researchers can confirm that pathway, they can then look for a way to break it.

The worst area for the botulism-related waterfowl deaths has been northern Lake Michigan, from Manistique, Michigan, east to the Mackinac Bridge and south down to near Frankfort, Michigan. Since 2006, a botulism outbreak has become an almost annual occurrence, but the outbreak of 2012 was unquestionably the worst so far. From mid-October to mid-November of that year, volunteers spread out across the area to search for carcasses of animals affected by botulism and discovered the carnage was vast. On the basis of their findings, researchers estimated that more than 1,000 loons died from the toxin, with 580 in Leelanau and Benzie Counties alone. Researchers also estimated the death totals for other species: 500 grebes, 500 long-tailed ducks, 500 double-crested cormorants, 250 white-winged scoters, and 250 gulls.

Given the way quagga and zebra mussels have increased water clarity and that they're not going anywhere anytime soon, that key factor contributing to botulism outbreaks is likely to remain constant for years to come.

Another result of the clearer water is an explosion of aquatic vegetation—what a layperson would call seaweed. The additional plant life means there are more hiding places for small fish, but it also makes boating and swimming less pleasurable. The biggest beneficiary of this shift appears to be cladophora, a genus of algae. The amount of cladophora in the lakes exploded in the 1960s, as it thrived in the phosphorous-rich human wastewater that was being pumped into the lakes at that time. Cladophora died back after phosphorous was removed from dish and laundry detergents and controlled in municipal sewage plants in the 1970s, but the algae have come back with a vengeance, benefiting from increased water clarity and an increase of phosphorous on the lake bed from mussel feces. A whole lot of mussels produce a whole lot of waste in the form of feces and pseudofeces, which is the stuff that mussels ingest and reject as inedible or undesirable. The net impact of all this mussel poop and pseudopoop has been to shift the available nutrient energy from the middle of the lake to the near shore benthic layer, benefiting shallow-water species like cladophora.

Cladophora grows naturally on hard surfaces such as rocks and logs in the lakes, and it's easily identifiable because it looks like long, flowing, green human hair. Summer storms, however, cause the lake to churn, and branches of the mature cladophora plants break off, float to the surface, and wash up on shore, creating a mat of green goo that smells like sewage. Although the cladophora itself is not harmful, it provides a place for bacteria to grow and often brings small crustaceans ashore, attracting large numbers of gulls looking for a meal.

The growth of all this cladophora has had two impacts. For humans, it has put a crimp on summer fun, as towns on Lakes Michigan and Huron are now forced to groom their beaches at least once a week to remove the stinky mat that look like lime-green gelatin. The other impact is on the organisms in the lake: all the nutrients that have been taken up by the cladophora have now been removed from the lake, transported to a landfill or compost pile, never to return.

———

Surprisingly, the two mussels have had a positive impact in a place where you might least expect it—lakeshore property values. A recent study by a student at the University of Wisconsin–Oshkosh found that property values in areas in central and northern Wisconsin rose 10 percent on inland lakes where zebra mussels were present, compared to inland lakes were they were not present.[2] The reason? The water was clearer. By contrast, property values fell approximately 4.5 percent on lakes with invasive Eurasian watermilfoil. Unfortunately, the mussels also make it more difficult to swim, as the shells are very sharp, therefore requiring any swimmers to don protective footwear.

———

As if all this isn't bad enough, the dreissenid mussels have the potential to do additional damage. In the same way that nutrients accumulate as they work their way up the food web, so do pollutants. As filter feeders, zebra and quagga mussels suck in anything small enough that floats past, including pollutants. In some places in the Great Lakes, the mussels have accumulated pollutants to a level more than three hundred thousand times greater than concentrations in the environment. Those pollutants, which include PCBs and polycyclic aromatic hydrocarbons, get transferred to any animal that eats a contaminated mussel. Those pollutants concentrate quickly in any predator that consumes several contaminated mussels.

Dreissenid mussels make up a good portion of the diet of adult round gobies, just like back in their native eastern Europe. But in this new ecosystem, the contaminants being consumed by gobies are being transferred and concentrated when they themselves are then eaten by Lake Erie northern water snakes.

Kristen Stanford's team at Ohio State University's Stone Lab has been drawing blood and collecting tissue samples from the water snakes and comparing them with samples taken before the arrival of the round goby. She has discovered that there has been an increase in biocontaminants found in the snakes, but so far at least, it has not become so much of a problem that it would interfere with reproduction.

———

The discovery of zebra mussels in North America is credited to Sonya Gutschi Santavy, who was at that time research assistant at the University of Windsor. Santavy was helping another researcher establish a research site in Lake St. Clair, near Detroit, in May 1988 when she brought up a sample from the lake floor that included something that looked like two rocks stuck together. Santavy was immediately suspicious and took the mussels back to the university for examination. Once the specimen was identified as a zebra mussel, researchers from the university set out to discover whether there were more and, if so, how widely they had spread. In July and August of 1988, they sampled areas around the lake to discover that the population was already out of control, leaving the researchers with the impression that the mussels had been in the lake for a handful of years before they were discovered. (Although Lake St. Clair gets credit for being the place where zebra mussels were discovered in the Great Lakes, there is evidence that they were found on a natural-gas wellhead on the Canadian side of Lake Erie in 1986.)[3]

With a rich abundance of food, the zebra mussel spread rapidly through the Great Lakes, carried by freighters, recreational boaters, and currents. The mussel population grew so dense in Lake Erie that it was estimated that in some places densities exceeded two hundred thousand individuals per square meter.

The quagga mussel, meanwhile, was a bit of a laggard. Although it was discovered in the Great Lakes only a year after the zebra mussel, it took much longer to spread. The zebra mussel had expanded its range all the way to the southern-most portions of Lake Michigan in 1990, but the quagga didn't appear in Lake Michigan until 1997. By 2007, however, the quagga mussel had become dominant in the Great Lakes, displacing the zebra mussel in many places. In fact, the quagga is now more widespread than the zebra ever was, with one form adapted to shallow water occupying nearshore areas and another morph adapted to deeper water occupying all offshore areas in all but the darkest depths. Quagga mussels have become so dense in Lake Michigan that it is estimated that there are about 450 trillion of them. To put it another way, there is now more quagga mussel biomass—the amount of living matter—in Lake Michigan than all the predatory fish combined.

This population density has all but wiped out native mussels in the Great Lakes. Prior to the arrival of dreissenid mussels, the Great Lakes and the Mississippi River had been centers for biodiversity for native mussels in North America. "Native mussels used to be abundant in Lake St. Clair and shallow Lake Erie," says Todd Morris, a mussel expert and research scientist at the Canada Centre for Inland Waters in Burlington, Ontario. Prior to the arrival of the dreissenid mussels, the open waters of Lake St. Clair had twenty native species; today, there are none. The natives disappeared in less than ten years due to direct competition.

There are a few scattered sites where native mussels still exist in the Lake St. Clair basin—up the Thames and Grand Rivers in Ontario and in the St. Clair River delta—but those populations are now isolated.

Now, with an elementary knowledge of mussels, a reasonable person might ask, "How does a mussel move up a river, counter to the water flow, if it is largely sedentary?" Unlike zebra mussels, native Great Lakes mussels go through a parasitic stage as juveniles. During this stage, they attach to the blood vessels inside the gills of a fish and feed. When the larva is just short of adulthood, it falls off and starts life as an adult, perhaps up a different river and often miles from where it originated. That means that Great Lakes tributaries are refugia for native mussels; it's possible for dreissenid mussels to reach these areas, but it's difficult without human help.

While the prospects may sound bleak for the native mussels, there are signs of hope. Dave Zanatta, a professor of biology at Central Michigan University, says even though freshwater mussels are the most imperiled group of organisms in North America, remnant populations appear to be thriving in water less than two meters deep with soft sediments and good wave action—all conditions that are unfriendly to the dreissenids.

While the native mussels have this one advantage over the invasives, the invasives have a huge advantage over the natives: numbers. An adult female zebra mussel can produce as many as one million eggs in a year. Once fertilized, the microscopic larvae—called veligers—will drift in water as plankton. It's likely that the mussels were transported to the Great Lakes as veligers and sucked into a ship with the ballast water. When they're three to four weeks old, often longer depending on the water temperature, the veligers settle and attach themselves to hard substrate and begin to feed by filtering plankton, calcium, and phosphorus out of the water. Calcium is particularly important for zebra mussel development, as that chemical element is necessary for a mussel to build its shell. The lack of calcium in water explains why the mussels have been slow to spread into the calcium-poor waters of Lake Superior.

Those areas might not be mussel-free much longer, however. There is evidence that the mussels are adapting to low-calcium waters. In 1999, zebra mussels were discovered underneath the pleasure-boat docks at Isle Royale National Park. Although it's possible that the mussels could drift to the island from shallower water in Minnesota, Wisconsin, or Michigan, the fact that they are being found under the docks and there alone makes it clear that boats are bringing the larvae in their live wells, ballast, or bilge water. That means the larvae are able to find enough calcium in the water to build their shells as they turn into adults.

Phyllis Green, the park's superintendent, says divers are sent out every summer to remove the mussels, which are brought to shore, crushed, bagged, and sent to a landfill. Because the mussels appear to be adapting to this calcium-poor water, Green now thinks there are two species on Earth that could survive nuclear Armageddon—cockroaches and zebra mussels.

———

The zebra mussel may have been discovered in Lake St. Clair, but it clearly found a comfortable home downstream in the western basin of Lake Erie. It was initially thought that zebra mussels would be unable to colonize western Lake Erie because they would be unable to live on the muddy lake bottom. But as the mussels spread, they changed the nature of the lake bed. As the first few mussels died and sank to the bottom, the next generation then settled on this new hard substrate.

That set the stage for crisis.

In 1989, Monroe, Michigan, became the first community in North America forced to deal with the dastardly zebra mussels. DTE Energy's Monroe plant is the second-largest coal-fired power plant in the United States and is the workhorse of the utility's coal-fired plants, providing power to more than two million customers in southeastern Michigan. Built on the western shore of Lake Erie, it has four units, each capable of generating 850 megawatts. To make the power, the plant must take in a million gallons of water *a minute* during the winter and 1.5 million gallons a minute in the summer. With that kind of intake, DTE Energy needed to be concerned about what was being sucked in—submerged logs, rope and other debris, and fish. Lots of fish. As many as one million three-inch gizzard shad could get sucked into the plant on a bad day. Solving the problem fell to a company task force led by William Kovalak, a DTE Energy biologist.

In 1988, Kovalak was working with commercial divers to relocate endangered native mussels on the Black River near Applegate, Michigan. One autumn Monday morning, two of the divers gave Kovalak an unidentified mussel attached to a rock. The divers told Kovalak that they had found it in the St. Clair River near Marysville, Michigan, during a pleasure dive the previous weekend. Even though he had never actually seen a zebra mussel, Kovalak was familiar with them from working with his mentor, Billy G. Isom, a biologist with the Tennessee Valley Authority (TVA). In the 1960s, Isom was dealing with invasive Asian clams in waterways in the southern United States as part of his job with the TVA. Based on research on Asian clams and other aquatic species, Isom determined that it was only a matter of time before zebra mussels arrived in North America.

He made that prediction in 1966.

Without knowing about the discovery made by Santavy just a few months earlier, Kovalak was surprised. He was even more shocked by the mussel's size. On the basis of its heft and the knowledge that zebra mussels grow slowly, he guessed that this particular individual had been in the river for three years or longer before being discovered. That meant that the introduction could have been as far back as the early 1980s.

When Kovalak went back to his office at the power-generating plant in Monroe, Michigan, he made it clear to his coworkers that in addition to solving the gizzard shad issue, they had a new, potentially much more serious problem—millions of mussels could soon be blocking the water-intake pipe. Immediately, Kovalak conducted a literature search to determine what they were up against. Meanwhile, the utility contacted a commercial diving team to inspect the water intake at the Monroe plant for a possible zebra mussel infestation.

The first inspection of the water-intake pipes in the fall of 1988 turned up only a handful of zebra mussels. But on the basis of an article about zebra mussel population dynamics in an invaded lake in Hungary, Kovalak estimated that the mussel population would expand tenfold over the next couple of years—which would be manageable.

If only that were the extent of the population growth.

The following year, divers again inspected the water intake and discovered the population had grown so dramatically that there were nearly eight hundred thousand mussels per square meter, and the buildup risked cutting water to the turbines. Kovalak says the zebra mussels expanded so rapidly because they bred twice in the same year in this nutrient-rich flow—something they had never been known to do before.

Kovalak and his task force went to work on a solution. They discovered that power plants in the United Kingdom had a similar problem with invasive zebra mussels, and their preferred treatment was to shut down the plant, close the water intake, scrape off as many as they could, and then treat the remaining mussels with chlorine to kill them. Kovalak says he and the task force spent many long hours searching for a more environmentally friendly solution than the toxic chlorine, but unfortunately the combination of scraping and chlorine worked best.

Of course, the zebra mussels caused additional unanticipated problems for the utility. Once the mussels were removed, they needed to be disposed of. Since the state would not let the utility send the mussels to a landfill, it was forced to send the mussels through a wood chipper and then put them on the power plant's property to compost—which almost immediately gave the utility another problem: the decaying mussels attracted a massive number of gulls that viewed the decomposing mussels as a smorgasbord.

On the other hand, the zebra mussels did hand DTE Energy one unexpected benefit: because the gizzard shad prefer cloudy water, they've been forced to move to deeper parts of the lake, and they no longer come close enough to get sucked into the plant.

———

At the same time that DTE Energy was struggling with its invasion of zebra mussels, the city of Monroe was dealing with a bigger problem.

In December 1989, a combination of zebra mussels and Lake Erie ice blocked the city's water intake, effectively cutting off drinking water to more than fifty thousand people in the city and the surrounding area for two and a half days.

Barry LaRoy is now the director of water and wastewater utilities for the city, but in 1990, he was an intern in the department. He remembers well watching his supervisors improvise solutions and scramble to make long-term plans to deal with a problem that nobody had ever dealt with before.

LaRoy was part of a team that installed a two-inch line to pump chlorine out to the water intake in Lake Erie. The constant flow of chlorine at the intake would kill the veligers and some of the adults living in the nine-mile-long pipe. Eventually, when the adults died at the end of their three-year life cycle, the pipe would be mussel-free.

The chlorine treatment was successful, but it caused other problems: dead mussels were now fouling the water plant; workers regularly removed bags and bags of mussel shells. Worse, the dead mussels gave the water a significant distasteful odor. In addition, the chlorine combined with decaying mussels caused a cancer-causing chemical to form in the water-intake pipe, requiring the plant to perform additional treatment.

The city spent more than $320,000 in 1989–90 to deal with the zebra mussel and was forced to spend more than $3 million to expand the water-treatment plant, build new groundwater wells, and link into a water-sharing system that provides drinking water to the southern part of the county.

The city continues to spend about $40,000 a year on zebra mussel treatment, but now that engineers know what they're doing, they know how to get away with doing just enough: the intake pipe is chlorinated only for about four weeks in the spring when the water temperature reaches fifty degrees to kill veligers and is chlorinated for four to six weeks again in the fall to kill any adults that may have settled in. "The setup we have now is the most cost-effective way of dealing with this at this point," LaRoy says. "There's a lot of science behind the decisions."

————

The cost of removing these mussels has led the managers at water facilities and power plants to ask whether there is some way to control or prevent the mussels.

Daniel Molloy was a research scientist at the New York State Museum Field Research Laboratory in the 1990s and was just wrapping up work on developing an environmentally safe biological control for the blackfly when he got a call from the New York Department of Environmental Conservation. Zebra mussels had spread into New York's waters on Lakes Erie and Ontario, and knowing that Molloy had developed a control for the blackfly, department managers wanted to know if he could develop a similar control for zebra mussels. Oh, and the utilities were willing to kick in $700,000 to get the process started.

Lacking any other direction, Molloy took a needle-in-the-haystack approach. He gathered bacteria from all over North America and grew them in the laboratory. Once he had enough for an application, he put them in water tanks filled with zebra mussels to see what would happen.

After three years of testing more than seven hundred different strains of bacteria, Molloy was discouraged, especially after having accepted an additional $5 million grant. Not having found a solution, he told the electric companies that they should cancel the contract and take the remaining money back because he felt it was unethical for him to continue to accept it without finding a result. Within a week, the companies responded. They told Molloy to keep plugging away.

Two months after Molloy told the power companies to cancel the contract, Molloy hit pay dirt with a bacterium in the genus *Pseudomonas*. "It was a moment that would bring tears to your eyes," he says.

Once Molloy was certain he had found a control for dreissenid mussels, he gave the bacterium to a company to have its DNA sequenced. It took more than a year, but the results identified the bacterium as *Pseudomonas fluorescens*.

Molloy will not reveal where he found the *Pseudomonas fluorescens* and plans to keep it a proprietary secret, but he does say that it originated in a North American river that already contained zebra mussels. Molloy says that *Pseudomonas* exists almost everywhere in relatively low levels, and in nature, it helps to protect plant roots from disease. But this specific strain, *Pf*-CL145A, is more than 90 percent effective in killing adult dreissenid mussels and 100 percent effective at killing larvae, but only if it occurs at levels high enough to be lethal.

Molloy spent the next ten years ensuring that *Pf*-CL145A would be safe for use, including testing it against native mollusks to ensure they would be unaffected.

With the work done, Molloy and the state of New York patented *Pf*-CL145A, and in 2007, it was licensed to Marrone Bio Innovations, a California company, to be sold as Zequanox.

Even though Molloy discovered that the bacterium kills dreissenid mussels, he will not make a penny on it because he did so in the role as an employee of the New York State Museum. All royalties from the licensing of his discovery will go to the state.

Zequanox has been successfully field tested in small, enclosed areas in California, Illinois, and Wisconsin. On a larger scale, in the fall of 2014 and winter of 2015, the Minnesota Department of Natural Resources appears to have eradicated zebra mussels from a 265-acre lake southwest of Minneapolis with a combination of Zequanox, copper, and potassium chloride. Although the department says that the result is not 100 percent conclusive, divers surveying the lake in April 2015 failed to find a single living zebra mussel.

Now that the EPA has approved Zequanox for "open water" use, it sounds like gallons of the stuff will soon be dumped into the width and breadth of

Lake Michigan. Unfortunately, Zequanox is not the silver bullet that will eliminate trillions of dreissenid mussels from the Great Lakes. Even though Zequanox has tremendous potential, it's economically unfeasible to attempt to control dreissenid mussels in a two-hundred-mile-long lake. However, its application will kill zebra and quagga mussels in small, shallow lakes and off docks, lake bottoms near beaches, or water intakes at power plants, which makes it a better *control* rather than eradication technique.

Zequanox is also far more effective than the previous chlorine treatments were; when the mussels sensed the caustic chemical, they simply closed their valves. When it comes to *Pf*-CL145A, however, the mussels do not realize they are ingesting a homicidal bacterium and stay open in its presence.

―――――――

The development and approval of Zequanox presents an amazing opportunity for wildlife managers, but it also presents a dilemma. As with any new technology, there are always questions about the best way to apply it. To explore those issues, the Great Lakes Commission, the US Geological Survey, the National Oceanographic and Atmospheric Administration, and the Great Lakes Fishery Commission formed a collaborative to explore the pros and cons of Zequanox or any other mussel-killing technology. Because zebra and quagga mussels are so widely hated, there are lots of people—lakefront property owners in particular—who are demanding that wildlife managers act immediately. The managers, however, are taking a cautious approach.

Even though it appears that Zequanox doesn't have an impact on native mussels, many questions remain. Is there an impact on the rest of the food web? What impact will those thousands or millions of dead mussels have on oxygen levels in the lakes since rotting organisms naturally deplete the oxygen level? The goal is to let science guide the wildlife managers and, at the same time, let the wildlife managers' need for information guide the science. That means that despite the availability of Zequanox, it will be a while before the product is applied in large amounts anywhere.

Even though Zequanox is a breakthrough in dreissenid mussel control, wildlife managers see it as just one part of an integrated pest-management plan with multiple options. The demand for additional control has Molloy back at work. Now that he has taken a research scientist position at the State University of New York at Albany, he's looking closely at a parasite that lives in European waterways and eats the mussels' connective tissues. It's possible, Molloy thinks, that this parasite could be introduced into the Great Lakes for basin-wide control.

Meanwhile, at Wayne State University in Detroit, a second possible control for dreissenid mussels is being developed by Donna Kashian and Jeffrey Ram. Kashian, a professor of biological sciences, and Ram, a professor of physiology in the medical school, have combined their knowledge and discovered chemical cues in algae that may be able to prevent the invasive mussels from breeding. Like Molloy's work with a parasite, Kashian and Ram hope their research can be used to disrupt zebra mussel breeding on a basin-wide scale. The key word is *disrupt*. Kashian and Ram view this only as a potential control, not an eradication technique.

Meanwhile, in Manitoba, wildlife managers are experimenting with applying liquid potash to kill zebra mussels. Early results from Lake Winnipeg were not promising; an application in May 2014 was fatal to native mussels, and larval zebra mussels were found in the treatment area just three months later. It was unknown how the larval zebra mussels came into the area; it's possible the larvae were part of a new infestation brought into the lake by a careless boater.

———

It's unlikely that Zequanox will ever be used as a widespread and effective way of controlling the zebra mussels, but there was one other method attempted: beer.

As a challenge to make a beer with only local ingredients, Excelsior Brewing Company on Lake Minnetonka, Minnesota, put zebra mussels and Eurasian watermilfoil, an invasive plant, in their Milfoil Lakehouse Saison Ale. According to a Minneapolis newspaper,[4] John Paul Awad, one of the brewers at Excelsior, developed the invasive-species ale after organizers of a local beer festival challenged brewers to make a brew using ingredients only from the state. Besides mussels and the milfoil, Awad included local honey and hops, as well as wild rice from the northern part of the state.

Even though the mussels are edible, the state of Minnesota advises against eating them because they can bioaccumulate pollutants. To prevent customers' livers from getting a double whammy, the brewers discard the meat of the mussels and only use the shells. The beer is also filtered prior to being bottled, so there's no chance of a shell ending up in the bottom of your shell.

Despite the unusual ingredients, the drink did not take on an unusual taste. "It ended up being a really great beer," Awad says.

Now, if it sounds like a cool idea to brew a sea lamprey and quagga mussel porter, here's a fair warning: don't. It is illegal to move invasive species, and Excelsior Brewing Company's attempt to make "lemonade" from a bad situation ended up with the brewery receiving a stern warning from the government.

———

So maybe there will never be a silver bullet that will offer widespread dreissenid mussel control, but there is a gray torpedo: the lake sturgeon.

The lake sturgeon (*Acipenser fulvescens*) is often referred to as a living fossil because it is a species that dates back 135 million years to the Upper Cretaceous period, which was also the peak of dinosaur development. The sturgeon has not changed much over that time, because unlike modern fish that are covered by scales, the sturgeon is covered with bony plates called scutes. The scutes grow in five rows along the body, two on each side and one on the back. On young fish, each scute comes to a peak with a sharp, thorny spur that protects young fish from predators. In older fish, the spurs have been worn down and are barely visible. An older sturgeon doesn't really need spurs because it is the largest fish in the Great Lakes. The lake sturgeon never stops growing, and with a life span that can stretch more than 150 years, it is capable of growing more than six feet long and weighing two hundred pounds or more.

Often residing in dark, murky water, the fish is a bottom feeder, using its four whisker-like barbels to detect food. When it finds food, it sucks it in with its tubular-shaped mouth and then takes in water to strain out sand and silt through its gills before swallowing.

And among the things that a lake sturgeon likes to eat are quagga and zebra mussels.

Michael Thomas, a fish biologist with the Michigan Department of Natural Resources' Lake St. Clair Fisheries Research Station in Harrison Township, Michigan, has been researching the diets of lake sturgeon since 1996 and says it is common to see the mussels in the sturgeon's digestive system. Thomas says lake sturgeon can eat mussels because they have an unusually thick, muscular stomach that allows them to easily crush the shells. That stomach also allows them to eat native mussels and invasive and native crayfish, snails, insect larvae, and plants.

The problem is, there aren't enough sturgeons in the Great Lakes to make much of a difference in the mussel population. Prior to European settlement, the sturgeon was one of the most abundant fishes in the Great Lakes. In the early nineteenth century, the sturgeon was perceived as a nuisance fish because it destroyed fishing nets; commercial fishermen wantonly killed sturgeon with every opportunity. Around 1850, however, commercial fishermen discovered the sturgeon had an economic benefit—it could be dried and used as fuel for steamboats. Numbers declined through the twentieth century, and by the 1990s, commercial harvest was no longer economical. By then, of course, the damage had been done: the population in Lake Erie alone had been reduced by an estimated 80 percent.

Besides being overfished, sturgeon numbers declined for two other reasons. First, many of the streams and rivers that the fish had used for spawning were dammed to make electricity. Second, the sturgeon population takes a long time to recover because it takes males twelve years to be mature enough to reproduce, and it takes females at least fourteen years.

As a result, the lake sturgeon is now considered threatened or endangered by many Great Lakes states and is listed as threatened in Ontario.

In response to the declining population, several organizations, including the Little River Band of Ottawa Indians based in Manistee, Michigan, are actively pursuing lake sturgeon restoration programs. Each spring, members of the tribe's Natural Resources Department go into the river to harvest lake sturgeon eggs and transport them into an enclosed tank. By removing the eggs and newly hatched larvae from the river, they are hoping to improve the fish's odds of survival. Every fall, the fish are removed from the tanks and released in the Manistee River in a community-wide ceremony. Instead of being transported to the river in large tanks and released into the river through a hose, the fish are placed in buckets and released into the river by hand.

The fish releasing has become an annual tradition in Manistee, says Allison Smart, an aquatic biologist with the tribe who is herself a member of the Sault Ste. Marie Tribe of Chippewa Indians. "It's a way for everybody to come together," Smart says. "Whether a tribal member or nontribal, it's a way of bringing people together. It's a ceremony to wish them well. Knowing that in twenty years that fish could come back to lay eggs is a special moment. You say your prayers and hope they make it."

———

If the mussels' invasion of the Great Lakes followed the pattern of most invasives, they would have peaked and seen their population fall back into equilibrium with their food supply. Twenty-five years into the invasion and with the amount of food diminished considerably, both mussels have begun to show signs of population decline but are nowhere near where biologists would expect them to be. That means that it will likely be some time before the influence of the mussels is diminished.

There's no question that the lakes have changed dramatically under the impact of the dreissenid mussels. But is it all bad? Yes, there are fewer fish in the lakes today because there is less plankton. Yes, the food web has been altered significantly, but plankton levels were artificially high, supported by massive amounts of nutrients added to the lakes through wastewater and runoff. So what do we want the lakes to be in the Age of the Dreissenid? "People look at lakes and want two things that are mutually exclusive," says Gary Fahnenstiel. "They want the water to look as clear as the water in a bathtub and there to be fish everywhere."

———

Water clarity and the food web aren't the only things altered by the zebra mussels. The mussels also changed policy toward invasive species as politicians reacted to the financial impact. Even though it was a back-of-the-envelope calculation, in 1989, Jon Stanley, who was the director of the US Fish and Wildlife Service's National Fisheries Research Center in Ann Arbor, Michigan, estimated that the zebra mussel would cost $5 billion in damage and control in the decade between 1989 and 1999. Months later, after having time to consider it more deeply, Stanley revised his estimate downward by a billion dollars, but the $5 billion figure had already galvanized Congress.

James Carlton, a professor of marine sciences at Williams College in Massachusetts, wrote that he believes that without Stanley's estimate of costs and damages, Congress would not have approved the Nonindigenous Aquatic Nuisance Prevention and Control Act 1990,[5] which was passed specifically to deal with the threat of the zebra mussels and created a national invasive-species task force to address the ballast-water pathway.

With the federal governments of the United States and Canada now closing the door on the introduction of organisms through ballast water, it was now time to find those other doors, and move to close them, too.

# 5

# CLAWS AND SPINES

It's a chilly, breezy, overcast August morning at the public boat launch in Elk Rapids, Michigan. Angry clouds stream across the sky in the wake of a line of strong thunderstorms and the passage of a cold front in the wee hours of the morning.

A five-member team from the Michigan Department of Natural Resources (DNR) prepares to launch two boats laden with dive and research gear as part of a study on the movements of rusty crayfish in the east arm of Lake Michigan's Grand Traverse Bay.

The smaller boat, which looks like a poor man's bass boat, is laden with three men, scuba tanks and other diving gear, and nets and bags. The bigger boat, a nineteen-foot Sea Ark, will be piloted by Randy Claramunt, a fisheries research biology specialist with the Michigan DNR in Charlevoix. Claramunt's boat is really nothing more than a giant hunk of molded and welded aluminum with a blunt nose that vaguely resembles a World War II landing craft. Even though the boat does not have a name, the team refers to it as the Love Boat because the driver's "seat," which is no more than a padded place to lean, is about the size of a loveseat. There are no other seats on board; anyone who wants to sit sits on either the floor or the gunwale. There's also no place to go to escape from the sun and no bathroom.

Claramunt noses the boat out of the slip and heads for open water to work on a research project tracking the movements of the invasive rusty crayfish. Today's destination is a reef just offshore that has been a center of Great Lakes research for decades. Claramunt says this reef was instrumental in helping the lake whitefish population recover after it crashed in the 1970s. There's still a cisco population here too; this is one of the few places in Lake Michigan where they are hanging on.

Because of the importance of this reef, researchers have come here over the past fifty years to study whitefish and cisco and also the impacts of invasive zebra mussels and round gobies. "This reef is a battlefield," Claramunt says.

Today, Claramunt and his team are back on this reef to study the movements of yet another invader: rusty crayfish. That crayfish army, along with a navy of invasive spiny water fleas, is now doing battle with native organisms trying to hold on. The natives, unfortunately, are on the verge of surrender.

―――――

The rusty crayfish and spiny water flea are both crustaceans, but they have little in common. Compared to the spiny water flea, which is about half an inch long and is barely visible to the human eye, the rusty crayfish is huge, growing more than four inches long. The crayfish has an exoskeleton, four pairs of walking legs, and two front legs with pincers for protection, fighting, and gathering food. When threatened by a potential predator, the rusty crayfish crouches down and shows off its pincers as a warning that it's not going to surrender without a fight. It was given its name for the rusty-colored spots on its back.

The spiny water flea, on the other hand, is not a flea or even an insect. It is in the order Cladocera and is one of more than six hundred species that are commonly called water fleas. The spiny water flea has four pairs of legs (which are often blue) that are used for capturing prey, antennae that are its primary means of movement, a piercing pair of mandibles for feeding that are half the size of its head, and one prominent eye that provides it with excellent eyesight. This water flea gets its "spiny" name from its pinkish-red tail, which makes up about 70 percent of the length of its body. In juveniles, that stiff tail features two prominent pairs of barbs, and in adults, there are three or four pairs of barbs. That long, needle-like tail and those barbs are important for self-defense because they prevent the spiny water flea from being eaten by small fish. A fish that is too small to fully ingest the water flea is likely to get the spine stuck in its mouth or have it puncture its stomach. To safely swallow a spiny water flea, the fish must be at least twenty times larger.

A set of pincers and a spiny tail with barbs help these two organisms when they are on defense, but it's their ability on offense that allows them to overwhelm their competition.

―――――

Unlike many of the other newcomers to the Great Lakes, the rusty crayfish didn't travel here from the opposite side of the world. The rusty crayfish

(*Orconectes rusticus*) is native to the Ohio River basin and was brought into the Great Lakes via three different pathways: the aquarium trade, the bait trade, and as science research subjects in elementary schools. These crayfish entered the wild when ignorant or otherwise well-meaning people released them. Ultimately, these releases are rich with irony for the following reasons:

- Aquarium owners often purchased rusty crayfish to increase the diversity of organisms in their tank. In the Great Lakes, however, rusty crayfish are reducing diversity.

- A science teacher should know better than to release a captive organism of dubious origin into a local stream or pond when it is no longer needed in the classroom.

- A crayfish intended to lure fish to an angler's hook is now having the effect of chasing fish away.

Anglers like to fish with the rusty crayfish because its thick exoskeleton can withstand being pierced by a fishing hook. That thick exoskeleton, however, makes these crayfish more difficult for any predator to digest.

The rusty crayfish is an opportunistic feeder and will eat everything from dead and decaying plants and animals to live aquatic plants, fish eggs, and small fish and invertebrates like mayflies, stoneflies, and midges. As a secondary consumer, it's at a level where it's going to eat and be eaten, just like native crayfish on the reef. The rusty crayfish is in direct competition with the three native crayfish species, and the invaders are winning. The rusty crayfish has a faster metabolism, so much faster that one biologist estimated that a rusty crayfish's caloric needs are twice as high as those of native crayfish species.[1] Simply put, the rusty crayfish are eating the native crayfish right off the reef.

Besides doing damage to native fish by eating their eggs, the rusty crayfish have caused the mass destruction of aquatic plant beds. In both the Great Lakes and smaller inland lakes, the crayfish have seriously reduced the abundance of aquatic plants that provide habitat for invertebrates, hiding spots for young fish, and food for certain other fish. The impact of the crayfish is particularly devastating in northern inland lakes, which are less productive, so they have a more difficult time recovering.

David Lodge, a professor of biology at the University of Notre Dame, compares the rusty crayfish to a lawnmower. While working at the University of Wisconsin, he watched the rusty crayfish turn an inland lake rich with plant life into something resembling a forest clear-cut in just a couple of years.

The two DNR boats anchor only a few hundred yards offshore in about four feet of water just north of Elk Rapids' harbor, so close you wonder why you even need a boat. Now it's time for Jason Buckley, a fisheries graduate student at Central Michigan University, to take charge. Buckley is here to investigate the movement of rusty crayfish by tagging them and following their movements. Buckley has established an underwater research site on the reef, and today it will be up to the divers to capture crayfish, bring them to Buckley to be tagged, and then return them to where they were captured.

This reef is full of rusty crayfish, so much so that the DNR set traps to remove them the previous year to help thin their numbers. That effort removed more than twelve hundred rusty crayfish, and based on what the divers will catch today, it seems as if there was no impact on the population.

On a previous trip, the divers laid down leaded lines on the lake floor to set up fifteen-by-fifteen-meter squares on the lake bottom to Buckley's instructions. Each box is divided into five-by-five-meter squares, so it looks like a giant tic-tac-toe board on the lake bottom. Divers then catch all the rusty crayfish in each square and bring them to the boat, where Buckley tags them and sends them back to be released in the area where they were found.

The divers catch the crayfish with their hands or a dip net and put them in small bags and bring to the boat. It's difficult work for the divers for two reasons: crayfish are fast and elusive, and they aren't afraid to use their pincers. Gloves help, but the divers still occasionally get a painful reminder of what they're catching.

The process for tagging is pretty simple: The crayfish are brought on board, and data are recorded for date captured, sex, and length. Buckley then attaches a floy tag, which is a long, thin, numbered piece of plastic with a notch in it. (The notch prevents the floy tag from falling out.) With each individual, he pushes a needle through two joints on the tail, which pulls the tag through until the notch is in place. Then excess plastic is cut off, and the crayfish is returned to where it was found. Only crayfish reaching fourteen-sixteenths of an inch or larger from head to the base of the abdomen are tagged. All others are considered to be too small. Buckley hopes to tag more than one thousand crayfish in this project.

The process of attaching a floy tag is slow and deliberate because even though Buckley is working with an invasive species, he doesn't want to risk injuring his study specimens. The process could have gone much more quickly if Buckley had decided to bring a soldering iron on board to brand the crayfish, but he decided not to bring a burning-hot tool on a rolling boat.

This portion of the reef is valuable to fish because it's composed of six feet of cobble-sized stone on top of a compacted clay substrate. The gaps between the stones allow fertilized fish eggs to fall deep into the cobble, where they

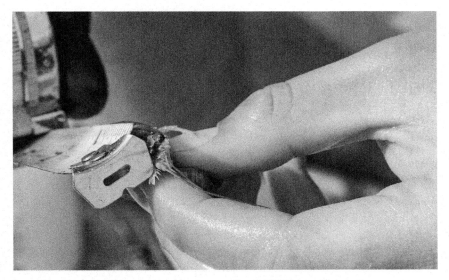

Jason Buckley, a fisheries graduate student at Central Michigan University, measures a rusty crayfish for his research project. Only crayfish that measure at least fourteen-sixteenths of an inch from head to abdomen were used in the study.

are protected from predators. Because it's shallow and relatively close to land, the water warms before the deeper water just a few feet away. In the spring, the young fish leave the safety of the cobble and swim to the shoreline to feed on the spring plankton bloom. The success of any year's whitefish population is critically tied to this nearshore nursery. If the food is good here, the young whitefish grow quickly and prosper. If for some reason the weather is cold or there is little food, the young whitefish will suffer.

As Claramunt explains the connection between the whitefish and the reef, a crayfish grabs onto one of Buckley's fingers. He flinches but resists the urge to shake his hand violently to get it off. "Ow, that hurts!" he says with a wince.

Claramunt quickly steps in to remove the crayfish with a secret weapon: the tip of his pencil. He drives the sharpened tip between the pincers and spins the pencil like he's driving a screw into wood. The conical shape of the pencil tip spreads the claw, and in a second or so, the crayfish drops off.

Claramunt returns to his side of the boat and sits back down on the gunwale. "Sharpened my pencil, too," he says with a wry smile.

———

Buckley is not alone in researching the rusty crayfish as an invasive. Although it's on a very different level, research on the rusty crayfish is part of the fifth-grade curriculum in Bob Thomson's fifth-grade class in Alpena, Michigan.

On a breezy, mostly cloudy, fifty-five-degree mid-May morning, a handful of Thomson's students stand in the cold water of the Thunder Bay River, dressed in chest-high waders and life jackets. Others scurry back and forth on the riverbank or look at aquatic organisms through microscopes. All of them seem oblivious to the chilly conditions.

Since 2007, Thomson has had his fifth-grade students out here in the river, fall and spring, learning about water-quality issues and invasive species. Each year, his students build three remotely operated vehicles (ROVs) equipped with motors, television cameras, and claws. The ROVs are neutrally buoyant, which allows the students to move the vehicles in all directions. The only limit on the ROVs' ability to move through the water is the length of the cable that connects them to the control.

The robotics aspect of this project started as an extracurricular activity when a group of students decided they wanted to enter into a competition sponsored by the Marine Advanced Technology Education Center, which is based in Monterrey, California. The activity was so popular that Thomson decided to make it a part of his regular curriculum. Now, every year the students spend part of their spring surveying the Thunder Bay River for invasive species. Their work is aided by the Great Lakes Stewardship Initiative, an organization that works in schools and communities to develop a new generation of environmental stewards.

When the students' yearly survey is done, they upload their data to the National Geographic FieldScope website, which is an interactive mapping platform that allows citizen scientists to document the natural world around them. The data gathered by the students help scientists to identify larger trends and answer important research questions. So far the students have documented rusty crayfish, zebra mussels, and an assortment of invasive plants in their river.

Even though the kids are here in the cold water of spring, they clearly love being outside, experimenting and having fun. Thomson says the fieldwork of his fifth-grade science curriculum starts the first week of school in the fall, and kids do research in the river right up until it freezes.

The children also now think of this as "their" river and work to keep it clean. On this particular morning, the students gather round a TV monitor on a table onshore to see that the ROV has found a skateboard in the river. It's now their self-appointed challenge to grab the skateboard with the ROV's claw and bring it to shore for proper disposal. Among the other things that the students have removed are aluminum cans, plastic bottles, and fishing lures.

Thomson believes the crayfish were introduced to the river by anglers upstream, and they have worked their way down to Alpena, displacing native crayfish along the way.

Crayfish are becoming a common learning tool for elementary school teachers—but they are not used the way Thomson uses them. Now, they're more like classroom pets that are used to teach biology. The use of live animals in classrooms has grown significantly since the start of the Great Recession in 2008. With that economic downturn, school districts decided there was no longer money in school budgets for field trips to local nature centers. With no money for trips, teachers turned to more classroom specimens, and the crayfish were big hits because the live animals helped teachers reach even the most recalcitrant learners. But at the end of the unit, teachers were left with a dilemma: what to do with the critters. For many, the solution was release.

Samuel Chan, a professor in fisheries and wildlife specializing in watershed health and an aquatic-invasive-species specialist for Oregon Sea Grant at Oregon State University, says he was made aware of the wild release of live animals after he was invited to a "spring release party" at a local elementary school. A spring release party might sound like a joyous occasion, but Chan was horrified to discover it was the day that the school released all its study specimens, including crayfish, into the wild.

What were these animals? Where did they come from? If these animals weren't native species, were schools unknowingly introducing animals into the wild that could become invasive? How could a classroom—a place of learning—be a source of invasive species and not even know about it?

Curious about the dangers of this pathway, Chan ordered crayfish from a biological supply house. A few days later, Chan received a box that again horrified him. The box contained red swamp crayfish, which are native to the southern United States, and a bag of Brazilian elodea, a plant that is so invasive that it is prohibited in several states. To make matters worse, there was no warning language about what he was receiving, and there were no instructions about proper disposal.

So if Chan received these two potentially invasive species in Oregon, what were teachers getting elsewhere? How widespread was the use of classroom specimens? Did schools have a policy for the disposal of these animals? With funding from the National Oceanic and Atmospheric Administration and Fisheries and Oceans Canada, Chan developed a survey and sent it to more than nineteen hundred teachers in several states and four Canadian provinces. From the responses, he learned that teachers often purchased organisms from a variety of sources, including supply houses, pet shops, and nurseries, but some teachers collected their own specimens from the wild.

Besides using crayfish, teachers used almost one thousand different types of animals in their classrooms, including fish, butterflies, and hamsters. Of those organisms, Chan discovered, 8 percent of them were considered invasive in the states to which they were shipped.

Chan learned that most of the classroom critters were given to students, other teachers, or people outside the district. Teachers also disposed of their classroom specimens by euthanasia, flushing them down a toilet, eating them, and putting them down storm drains. Many of the classroom critters died on their own.

Because many teachers, students, and parents balked at the idea of euthanasia, about 27 percent of the classroom specimens were released into the wild. Chan believes it is likely that a high percentage of the organisms that were given to children also ended up being released into the wild.

Part of the problem, Chan says, was that biological supply houses did not believe it was their responsibility to educate the teachers on the proper disposal of their specimens. Since his survey and education and outreach efforts, both the teachers and biological supply houses that he has contacted have pledged to make changes to lower the risk.

––––––

Even though people across North America are working to educate and hopefully lower the risk of future introductions, Jason Buckley is in the here and now on his rusty crayfish work, and it appears it's going to be a long day. By midmorning, the wind has started to shift to the west, and the bay is now getting choppy—there are no whitecaps yet, but the waves are growing. It's not a good sign since there are several more hours of work yet to do.

Nevertheless, the flow of crayfish does not slow. There used to be perhaps anywhere between two and five native crayfish per square meter on this reef. Now, it's estimated there are as many as thirty rusty crayfish per square meter, and native crayfish are nearly impossible to find. Although there are no definitive data, Claramunt believes based on observation that the rusty crayfish numbers decline over the course of a summer because they compete with round gobies for food. Even though the gobies can eat more than the crayfish at warmer lake temperatures, the gobies barely eat during winter. Those temperatures, however, do not stop the crayfish from eating. During winter, the gobies will also leave the reef for warmer water, and the crayfish numbers explode again.

Eric Calabro, a Michigan DNR research technician who is one of the divers today, says that he once saw three gobies attacking a rusty crayfish to chase it from an area that they wanted. In fact, the gobies are so aggressive toward the rusty crayfish that Calabro has seen gobies turn over a rusty crayfish to eat the young that were attached to the underside of their parent.

A rusty crayfish rests on a rock on a Grand Traverse Bay reef after being tagged for a research project.

Now there is new concern about yet other potential invasives—the red swamp crayfish and the yabby. The red swamp crayfish species is native to the US South and is a staple of Louisiana cooking. Although it's legal to import them into northern states to be sold as food, anglers are purchasing them as bait, and schools are receiving them for classroom use. And as with the rusty crayfish, anglers are releasing their excess red swamp crayfish into the wild at the end of the day. Recent discoveries in a Wisconsin inland lake and a Michigan river show that these crayfish are hardy enough to survive a cold northern winter. The yabby, meanwhile, is a highly desired crayfish in the aquarium trade in Australia because it has been bred to be a beautiful shade of blue. Despite the aesthetics, in 2014, the state of Michigan made it illegal to possess a yabby.

Why ban it? The biggest clue comes in the yabby's scientific name, *Cherax destructor*, because the yabby will kill and eat just about anything it can find.

There's really no way to check the rusty crayfish population through chemical or biological controls, so maybe the best technique for controlling it is gastronomic. Largemouth bass and other fish eat the crayfish, but so do humans.

One study published in 2007 showed that trapping was successful in reducing rusty crayfish in one inland location by about 95 percent,[2] and in 2009, students at the University of Wisconsin removed about one hundred thousand rusty crayfish from one inland lake. Instead of tossing those

A Michigan DNR employee returns rusty crayfish to the Grand Traverse Bay reef, where they were captured. The crayfish were tagged as part of a study that tracked crayfish movement.

crayfish into a landfill to be consumed by gulls, the students turned those crayfish into jambalaya and other Louisiana-style dishes.

It appears that rusty crayfish are becoming part of the human diet all across the Upper Midwest. One seafood restaurant in Minneapolis now has rusty crayfish on the menu, and one food market there now carries rusty crayfish in its frozen food section. To help anybody experimenting with the dish, a Minnesota Sea Grant webpage offers several recipes for preparing rusty crayfish, including fried crayfish tails and kraftor, a Swedish recipe that includes lots of dill.[3]

Unlike the rusty crayfish, the spiny water flea came to North America from its native range in northern Europe and Asia, likely introduced through ships' ballast water. *Bythotrephes longimanus* was discovered in Lake Ontario in 1982 and was subsequently found in Lake Huron in 1984, Lake Erie in 1985, Lake Michigan in 1986, and Lake Superior in 1987.

Like the rusty crayfish, the spiny water flea has an impact on both ends of the food web, eating zooplankton and being eaten by larger fish. And like the rusty crayfish, its impact has been dramatic: it is responsible for reducing the biomass of microcrustaceans by half.

*Bythotrephes* is common in its home range but far less dominant than it has become in the Great Lakes. Eurasian zooplankton can often escape; they are able to sense when a spiny water flea is near because they can detect either a chemical cue in the water or a pressure wave from the approaching predator and escape. But many native zooplanktons cannot detect the water flea because they are unfamiliar with this newcomer's chemical cue; they have no idea that a predator is about to pounce.

The only zooplankton that seems to have escaped the wrath of the water flea is *Daphnia mendodia*, which is now the only member of the daphnia family left in Lake Michigan, says Norman Yan, a biology professor at York University in Toronto. *Daphnia mendodia* is able to sense the spiny water flea's pressure wave and dives into deeper, darker water. The water flea, being a visual hunter, is unable to find its prey in the dark. Because the spiny water flea is always lurking, the daphnia have changed their behavior and now stay deeper in the lake during daylight hours.

Charlie Kerfoot, a professor at Michigan Technological University in Houghton, Michigan, says as an experiment, he put native zooplankton in a tank with *Bythotrephes* to see what would happen. Kerfoot says it was shocking how quickly the native plankton got wiped out. "They were blind-sided," Kerfoot says. "They just didn't realize there was a threat."

Donn Branstrator, a biology professor at the University of Minnesota–Duluth, began work on his doctorate at the University of Michigan in the fall of 1987, shortly after the discovery of spiny water flea in the Great Lakes. Branstrator says studying the water flea was a natural choice and a rare opportunity because it was new to the ecosystem and its impacts would be transmitted both up and down the food web.

The other thing that attracted Branstrator was the water flea's size: compared to other freshwater zooplanktons, the water flea is like a grizzly bear—more than twice as large.

When the spiny water fleas enter a lake, they reduce the abundance and biodiversity of zooplankton. But, Branstrator says, it's still unknown what that change in the balance of zooplankton means, if anything, for plankton-eating fish.

Larger fish, however, can gorge on the spiny water flea. The smallest populations of *Bythotrephes* are found in Lakes Superior and Ontario. In Superior, it appears that the cisco population keeps the water fleas in check, and in Ontario, it appears that the alewives are doing the job. In inland lakes, it appears that the pumpkinseed is the biggest predator. Although the pumpkinseed is not that large, it has the unusual ability to move its jaw muscles so that it can separate the water flea's tail from its body and spit out the tail. It can do this because it has specially adapted muscles and teeth strong enough to crush the shell of a snail, which is part of its normal diet.

Yan says those fish that are able to eat the water flea are getting a nutrient-rich food item, and in the course of his research, Yan says he has caught fish with their stomachs full of the crustacean.

Fish are likely to be the best natural control for the spiny water flea because, unlike the rusty crayfish, human consumption is unlikely. Yan calls himself an applied biologist because he is interested in researching questions that can solve a problem and have an immediate impact. But even he admits that he may have gone a bit too far in his research when he once chewed on a handful of spiny water fleas in an effort to understand what impact they might have on a fish trying to eat them. He compared the experience to chewing on straight pins.

————

*Bythotrephes*, besides wielding an epee on the end of its body, has one other trick that allows it to spread rapidly: its eggs cannot be digested in a fish's guts. The eggs have a thick shell that allows them to pass through a fish and still be viable. Therefore, a spiny water flea's eggs end up spreading from place to place—perhaps by the thousands or hundreds of thousands every year—in the guts of fish because anglers often catch small fish in one lake and use them as bait in another. Or perhaps the fish defecate the eggs into a boat's live well, and the angler empties the water and the eggs into a lake at the end of the day.

Even though the eggs are tough enough to withstand a gut, they might just be the weakness that will lead ultimately to control of *Bythotrephes*. The eggs will die if they are removed from water and allowed to dry. Ultimately, Branstrator says, that may be what keeps the organism from spreading from lake to lake. If boaters allow their watercraft and fishing gear to dry completely before moving them to another lake, the odds of preventing transfer go way up.

Other ways boaters can help are never to dump water from a bait bucket into a lake, because spiny water flea eggs may be in the bottom, and never to clean a caught fish near the water, because the water flea's eggs may be in the fish's digestive system.

Yan believes *Bythotrephes* eggs have one other weakness: they live for only two years unhatched. If some method could be found to prevent the spiny water fleas from breeding for three or more years, a lake potentially could be free of them.

————

It's now early afternoon on Grand Traverse Bay, and the divers are starting to lag. After they have collected more than one hundred crayfish from two different study sites, it's time to call it a day. Showing their fatigue, the divers crawl on their boat and drop off their tanks. Today's battle is done, but the war is by no means over. On the trip back to the dock in Elk Rapids, Claramunt and Buckley start making plans to return to this spot later in the month for another dive to collect the tagged crayfish.

Buckley's project is just one small part of the war on invasive species. The information gained from his research and other similar projects will help biologists and wildlife managers make good decisions on control efforts. Those control efforts are unfortunately years off in the future. In the here and now, policy makers and wildlife managers are picking a new fight, and it's surprisingly close to home.

# 6

# THEN CAME HYDRILLA

Lake Manitou is one of the gems of Indiana's inland lakes.

The lake's shoreline is crammed with six hundred houses, ranging from one-bedroom cottages to beautiful mansions. There are also condominiums, a marina, and a restaurant. Many of the people who live on this north-central Indiana lake were lured there by the great fishing, and nearly everybody owns a boat.

Unfortunately, nonresidents love Lake Manitou also. As one of the largest bodies of water for miles around, the 735-acre lake is often overrun on weekends by boaters with powerful ski boats and wave runners. On summer weekends and holidays, it gets so crowded that residents avoid going out—there are just too many boats in too small an area.

The lake's popularity caused another problem: an infestation of Eurasian watermilfoil, an invasive aquatic plant that is native to Europe and Asia. It's widely despised by boaters and swimmers everywhere because it spreads rapidly, grows in dense mats on the surface in shallow areas, and makes boating difficult and swimming uncomfortable.

Eurasian watermilfoil (*Myriophyllum spicatum*) has become a major problem in the Great Lakes basin. Introduced into the United States through the aquarium trade, the plant was first found in the wild in a pond in Washington, DC, in 1942. In 1949, the plant was found in Lake Erie at Put-in-Bay, Ohio, and has since spread into the western United States. In the Great Lakes, it can be found in bays and marinas and other places with slow-moving water. It spreads easily because plant fragments in one lake can be carried by a boat, by a trailer, or even attached to the feet or feathers of a duck or goose and can establish in another lake. Eric Fischer, the invasive-species coordinator for the state of Indiana, says Eurasian watermilfoil was likely introduced to Lake Manitou as far back as 1987 on a boat or trailer of a weekend visitor who brought it from another lake. If the conditions are right, Fischer says, the plant can stay viable out of the water for as long as five days.

The plant may have been introduced into Lake Manitou by one of those weekend boaters, but it became the property owners' problem. Within a few years of the discovery of Eurasian watermilfoil, the surface of the lake's shallow areas was covered with a dense mat of green weeds. Boaters found it difficult to navigate all but the deepest portions of the lake. Just getting a boat to and from a dock became difficult, and boat owners trying to navigate through the weeds risked having their motors clogged and destroyed. If it was tough to get a boat through this tangle, the simple and joyous act of jumping off a dock on a summer afternoon became something to avoid.

In 2005, homeowners decided to tackle the issue head-on. Working closely with the state, the homeowners' association hired a company to apply herbicide to control the milfoil. The state, meanwhile, started regular surveys of the lake to ensure that the milfoil was being killed but that other plants and wildlife weren't being harmed. It was on one survey in August 2006 that the biologists found a small piece of another invasive plant, hydrilla.

Even though it was just a tiny fragment, it was enough to set off alarm bells across the Great Lakes region.

―――――

Biologists call hydrilla "the perfect plant." It is native to Africa, Asia, and Australia, and came to North America in the aquarium trade in the late 1950s. The whorls of leaves along its long stem make it an attractive plant, and its ability to grow in nutrient-poor water make it highly desirable for owners of aquariums and backyard ponds.

Unfortunately, however, aquarium and backyard-pond owners looking to get out of the hobby all too often dump the contents of their aquariums and water gardens in a nearby lake or stream, thinking that it's better than flushing them down a toilet. Nobody knows for certain, but it's believed that if the hydrilla wasn't transported into the lake on a boat trailer, an aquarium or pond owner was responsible for the infestation in Lake Manitou.

In North America, hydrilla grows in two forms—one that is happy in the heat of the US South and one tough enough to withstand the harsh winters of New England and the Midwest. It grows rapidly—up to an inch a day—and can reproduce four different ways: through seeds, fragments, new plants from the roots, and turions, which are highly specialized bulbs built to survive subfreezing temperatures.

Hydrilla sales are now illegal in all of the Great Lakes states, but the plant still sneaks into backyard ponds when plants are harvested in the wild in Florida. Fischer says it has been proven that on occasion hydrilla tubers are found in the soil of those pond plants. The shippers do not inspect every plant sold, so it is up to buyers to wash the roots of their plants prior to installation to make sure there isn't a stowaway hydrilla tuber. But most plant buyers are hesitant to wash away the soil, Fischer says, because they don't want to risk damaging the roots. And it may not be immediately apparent that the pond owner got a bonus plant, as hydrilla tubers can sit for years before sprouting.

Hydrilla is considered the most serious aquatic weed problem in Florida and is a major problem in many waterways in the southern United States. It was a bigger threat to Lake Manitou for the following reasons:

- Hydrilla can grow in water up to thirty feet deep. Eurasian water-milfoil does not grow more than fifteen feet long and cannot grow in water more than twenty feet deep. Hydrilla could have turned Lake Manitou into a mat of plants so thick that a duck would have been able to walk from shore to shore.

- Eurasian watermilfoil grows densely, but hydrilla grows denser, sending out multiple branches from one stem. If boating was difficult because of milfoil, hydrilla would have made it impossible.

- Unlike milfoil, hydrilla is able to grow on more substrates and in nutrient-poor water.

If Eurasian watermilfoil choked Lake Manitou, hydrilla would swallow it whole.

———

Lake Manitou's infestation was not the first time hydrilla was found in the Midwest. In 1972, hydrilla was introduced to an ornamental pond in Iowa and was later eradicated. Indiana officials wanted to eradicate it in Lake Manitou, of course, but they also wanted to be sure it did not spread and reach the Great Lakes. Equally important, Indiana did not want it to spread into the rivers and canals in the northern part of the state that carry billions of dollars of goods on barges between Lake Michigan and the Mississippi River. If hydrilla were to reach the Calumet River or the Cal-Sag Channel, it could easily spread unchecked into countless rivers in a watershed that covers two-thirds of the North American continent.

(Since the discovery of hydrilla in Lake Manitou, the aquatic weed has been found in multiple places near Cleveland in northeastern Ohio; in the Ohio River in West Virginia, Ohio, and Kentucky; and in the Erie Canal near

North Tonawanda, New York. In July 2014, the US Army Corps of Engineers began to treat a fifteen-mile stretch of the Erie Canal and Tonawanda Creek with the goal of eradication. The Ohio DNR monitors the plants in the Ohio River but admits nothing can be done about them other than to ask boaters to ensure their boats and trailers are weed-free after exiting the water.)

The Indiana DNR immediately set up a series of community meetings to explain the problem and, more importantly, the steps that would be taken to prevent the spread. Given the large amount of boat traffic in and out of the lake and its location only seventy miles from Lake Michigan, the decision was made to close the lake to all nonresidents and to severely restrict home-owners' ability to remove and relaunch their watercraft.

Although a few homeowners objected, many of the property owners were thrilled to have the lake shut down to outsiders. What they did not care for were the restrictions on their ability to remove and return their boats any-time they wanted. Boats could be launched in the spring and removed only for repair or for winter storage.

"We spent a lot of time with the lake owners' association and went through the rationale and what needed to be done," Fischer says. "There was resistance to a lake-wide shutdown but not as much as you might imagine. The property owners did not want to lose property values."

Over the next seven years, the Indiana DNR spent $2 million to treat every square inch of the lake, dumping in barrel after barrel of Sonar, an aquatic herbicide that costs $1,600 a gallon, plus a granular version of the same chemical. The treatment essentially turned the lake into a vegetation-free moonscape.

In 2013, the DNR began to scale back the treatment to the area where hydrilla was found in 2006. Finally, in 2014, after spending $2 million, the DNR reached a milestone after divers conducting an annual plant survey for the DNR failed to find a single hydrilla plant. The DNR is hesitant to declare victory, however. It can do that only after years of monitoring Lake Manitou and if other nearby lakes show no additional infestations.

———

Indiana's reaction to the discovery of hydrilla demonstrates two changes in invasive-species management. First, instead of opting for control, govern-ments now emphasize prevention and early identification and rapid response for eradication. Second, although ballast water is still the top priority because it's still the largest potential pathway, the prevention effort has widened to include the pet trade, backyard ponds, the sale of bait, and recreational boating.

Governments across the Great Lakes basin now emphasize prevention and eradication because they have learned over the past thirty years that it is

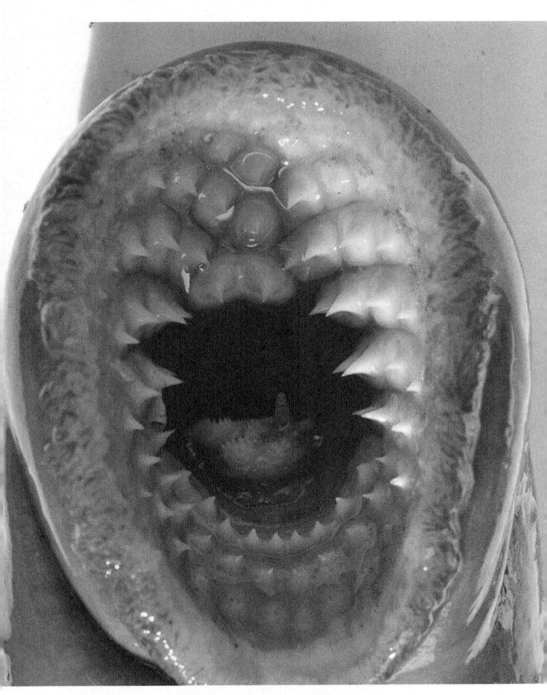

The sea lamprey's mouth is a whorl of teeth that are used to grip and scrape away at a fish's scales so that its tongue can dig deeper into a fish's body to suck out blood and other bodily fluids. The teeth themselves are made of keratin, similar to an adult's fingernails.

Adult round gobies prey on zebra mussels in the Great Lakes, similar to the way the fish consume the mussels in their native range in eastern Europe. Some biologists believe that the round goby likely would have had a much more difficult time establishing itself in the Great Lakes if not for the presence of zebra mussels as an easy source of food.

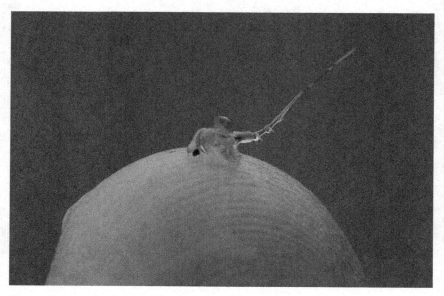

The spiny water flea is small enough to fit on the tip of a human finger, but its spine can puncture the stomach of and ultimately kill any small fish that tries to digest it.

Invasive rusty crayfish are larger than native Great Lakes crayfish species and are therefore able to dominate them when it comes to finding food and competing for the best spots to breed.

Eurasian watermilfoil growing in a laboratory at Grand Valley State University's Annis Water Resources Institute in Muskegon, Michigan. Researchers are working to learn more about the plant's biology in an attempt to find a weakness they can exploit that may lead to better control or eradication.

Blake Bushman, a natural resource coordinator with the Illinois Department of Natural Resources, removes a silver carp from a gill net. The carp had been caught in the Illinois River as part of an effort by the Illinois DNR to fish down the population and potentially prevent an invasion of the Great Lakes.

smarter and far less expensive to prevent species from entering an ecosystem than it is to try to control them after they are established.

"I remember when I took this job, my boss said that when it comes to invasives, it's prevention, prevention, prevention," says John Navarro, the aquatic-invasive-species program administrator for the Ohio Department of Natural Resources Division of Wildlife. "Close those vectors. . . . If we could just keep these things out, we'd be saving so much money and resources."

Until recently, the focus of invasive-species research and control has been on individual species. But in a society where people and goods move quickly around the globe and organisms can be purchased easily over the Internet, the focus has shifted to identifying and closing off potential pathways for additional introductions. That is a challenge that has many forms, and efforts to prevent introduction are only as good as the least effective regulation.

——

In the four years between 2005 and 2008, the United States legally imported more than 1.4 billion ornamental fish. Again, 1.4 billion.

Although many of these four thousand species are benign, Michael Hoff, a regional invasive-species coordinator with the US Fish and Wildlife Service (FWS) in Minnesota, believes that when it comes to the potential damage, our eyes are wide shut. That's because current federal law allows the legal importation of a species until it is considered injurious and is listed as illegal to import under the federal law that governs the importation of plants and animals, the Lacey Act of 1900. Unfortunately, Hoff says, under the Lacey Act, an imported species is considered innocent until proven guilty. The problem is, of course, that by the time it's proven guilty, it's too late. What's worse, it's difficult to get an organism listed as injurious. In 2013, US Rep. Joseph Heck (R-NV) introduced a bill in Congress to make the importation and shipment of quagga mussels illegal. The bill died when the congressional session ended in December 2014; the bill was never even brought up for a vote in a House subcommittee.

Hoff points out that among those species that can still legally be imported into the United States under current rules are the stone moroko (*Pseudorasbora parva*), the zander (*Sander lucioperca*), and the giant tigerfish (*Hydrocynus goliath*). There are well-documented cases of the zander and the tigerfish attacking humans in Europe and Africa, respectively, and Hoff believes all three are dangerous to the Lake Michigan ecosystem in particular.

The good news is, even if Congress won't do its job, federal agencies can make some rules without having to seek additional authority from Congress. In 1999, President Bill Clinton signed an executive order mandating the development of a federal invasive-species management plan and for federal agencies to use their authority to prevent the introduction of invasives.

Hoff equates government progress to dog years—something that should take one human year ends up taking the government seven, and that includes the rule-making process. "It makes infinity look short," Hoff says.

With little movement on the president's executive order, in 2010, Secretary of the Interior Ken Salazar again asked FWS to develop a risk-assessment plan. The request was eventually dropped on Hoff's desk, and it couldn't have found a better place. Hoff is a rare public servant—energetic, visionary, savvy, and dedicated—and he immediately got to work on a way of assessing and managing risk from exotic species.

For three years, Hoff worked to adapt Climatch, a screening method developed in Australia that uses a scoring method to determine how likely a species is to find a similar climate and habitat outside its native range. Hoff adapted that screening method to North America to create the Risk Assessment and Mapping Program (RAMP), with the goal of identifying species that are likely to become invasive so they can be prohibited for import into the United States. In just a few hours, the screening process can produce a comprehensive report about a species's ecological risk.

The RAMP process flips the Lacey Act's innocent-until-proven-guilty approach but avoids unnecessary regulations on the pet industry and the aquarium or backyard-pond trade that would affect the importation of low-risk species.

Although the pet industry and FWS have often been at odds over the past twenty years, the two have signed a memorandum of understanding that voluntarily commits the industry to avoid importing high-risk species. FWS, however, continues to see evidence that some individuals want unusual and exotic species, and Internet message boards for aquarium enthusiasts are full of requests from people seeking unusual fish. Two of the species that turn up often on these message boards are wels catfish and Nile perch—species that may well end up in the wild when their owners realize that buying either one was a *bad* idea. Wels catfish, which are native to southern and central Europe, can grow up to thirteen feet long and weigh more than four hundred pounds, and really, no casual hobbyist has a tank large enough to contain something that big.

———

But what about individuals who are looking to sell organisms in their aquariums? Do the private dealers who conduct their business on Craigslist and eBay know that it's illegal to ship a pacu to certain states?

To educate sellers, the Great Lakes Commission in 2012 developed the Internet Sales of Invasive Species Detection System, a web crawler that searches the Internet for high-risk and restricted organisms for sale. The software helps give biologists, wildlife managers, and law enforcement a way to monitor this pathway for invasive species. In a matter of a few seconds, the software can turn up a list of organisms for sale on the Internet that are considered to be high risk to the Great Lakes, including

- a trapdoor snail being sold on eBay;

- aquatic plants and Malaysian Trumpet Snails on Craigslist; and

- parrot's feather—an aquatic plant—offered for sale by an Internet-based business.

Some web dealers are aware that it is illegal to ship to certain states and make it clear where they will not ship, but according to Erika Jensen, a project manager for the Great Lakes Commission, the information on those websites is often incomplete or incorrect.

So what should an aquarium owner do with an unwanted, potentially invasive organism? One pet store in Milwaukee believes it has a simple solution: give it to us. Hoffer's Tropic Life Pets in Milwaukee, Wisconsin, isn't just a pet store; it's a destination. Yes, people come to shop, but they also come just to wander the aisles and look at the amazing displays. The shop regularly hosts birthday parties, and school groups come in for live animal presentations. Because of the store's role in the community, Joe Olenik, its fish-room manager, says its managers have a wider sense of responsibility. Olenik and storeowner Mike Hoffer concluded that they needed to know more after an outreach person from the Habitattitude campaign discovered that the store had a restricted plant for sale.[1]

Not only has the store begun to carefully monitor what's offered for sale, but Olenik has also taken a new attitude toward his customers. He now tries to match customers with certain species and products that fit their lifestyles to help ensure they are making good choices. And he's not above turning buyers away if they are interested in inappropriate or illegal species, earning him the nickname the Fish Nazi. It's a title he is comfortable with. "Just because somebody can afford to buy an animal doesn't mean they should," Olenik says.

When the recession hit in 2008, many people began to come into the store looking to unload plants and animals that they could no longer afford. Olenik will take the organisms in and put them back on sale if he can. In the case of exotic pets, however, Olenik says he'll take the organism, but he makes it clear to the customer that it will be euthanized. "I can count on two hands the number of days of the year when I don't take something in from the public," Olenik says. "We let people know, 'If you don't want it, bring it here. Do not release into the wild.'"

For years, the Shedd Aquarium, on the Lake Michigan shore just south of downtown Chicago, had ignored the failing ecosystem right outside its back door, choosing instead to feature displays about flashy tropical fish and dying coral reefs in faraway oceans.

Around 2005, the aquarium decided to make the Great Lakes a priority and renovated the Great Lakes Gallery to bring in little-known native species such as the cisco and burbot and invasives such as the sea lamprey and silver and bighead carp. But educating the public is a daunting task, says Jim Robinett, the senior vice president of external and regulatory affairs at the Shedd. Illinois has only sixty-three miles of shoreline on Lake Michigan, and most of the people in the state identify more with the prairie than with the water.

As if to illustrate the gap that Robinett faces, the wall behind him in the conference room has a photo of dolphins performing a trick in front of an excited audience in his aquarium. That's the challenge that Great Lakes advocates face: a burbot or a cisco can't compete with a dolphin's charisma, and it's difficult to get people worried about the loss of something called a slimy sculpin.

Robinett, however, thinks the lake sturgeon can become the charismatic poster child for the Great Lakes, and the aquarium has opened a sturgeon touch tank to let children touch the unusual bony plates that cover the fish's body.

More than two million people visit the Shedd Aquarium annually, and as it is the largest aquarium in the country, Robinett likes to think of it as an aquatic zoo. People come to see the colorful fish, "but if we can sneak a little education on them, the better."

———

Four hundred and fifty miles to the northwest, on the steep hills of Duluth, Minnesota, Doug Jensen, the aquatic-invasive-species coordinator with Minnesota Sea Grant, is dissatisfied with such a passive effort. Tourism is an $11 billion industry in Minnesota, and 266,000 jobs are connected to it. Nearly 20 percent of Minnesotans say they fish, and 36 percent of tourists participate in fishing. Minnesota has a lot to lose from the impact of invasive species. With that motivation, Minnesota Sea Grant has been working aggressively at outdoor shows, trade shows, and seminars to educate people about the importance of stopping the spread of exotic species.

Minnesota was the first state to outlaw the transportation of aquatic plant species, and based on surveys taken around the state, the message has gotten through. More than 96 percent of boaters say they are willing to clean their boats and trailers, drain their live wells, and dry their boats for at least

A sign at a boat launch in Michigan's Upper Peninsula urges boaters to take precautions against spreading invasive species via their boats and trailers. States in the Great Lakes region are asking boaters to cooperate because it is easier and better to prevent the spread of invasives than it is to try to control them after they have spread to new locations.

five days before transferring the boat to a different lake. Two different surveys showed that nine out of ten people knew about the state's Stop Aquatic Hitchhikers campaign. Those surveys also showed that 85 percent of the anglers said they had been personally affected by aquatic invasives at some level already, and 97 percent of people felt personally responsible for helping to maintain the quality of the lakes. Jensen says the surveys showed that less than 2 percent of the boaters don't care if they were responsible for the spread of invasives. Those who did not care said they believed that invasive organisms were going to spread anyway, so why should they try to do anything about it? One reason: to avoid stiff penalties. Boat owners can be fined if they fail to clean their boat and trailer properly, and inspectors at launch ramps can prevent people from launching a boat if it fails to pass inspection.

The state of Wisconsin, concerned about the spread of invasive species by its own employees, has developed an "everything is everywhere" approach when it comes to cleaning boats, trailers, and gear owned by the state's Department of Natural Resources. Wisconsin has three invasive species in inland lakes—the Asian clam, New Zealand mud snail, and faucet snail—that have yet to find their way into the Great Lakes. Wisconsin has discovered that the two snails are able to move from lake to lake not just on boats but on objects like waders and fishing nets. That's because the two snails are so small that they can often evade detection. Even if they are detected, they are difficult to deal with because they can survive the traditional disinfection treatments of power washing a boat and trailer with a solution of hot water and bleach or Virkon, a common disinfectant that contains potassium peroxymonosulfate, sodium dodecylbenzenesulfonate, and sulfamic acid. The only way to ensure that both snails are killed is to power wash a boat and gear for five minutes with boiling water. And since the New Zealand mud snail reproduces asexually and the Asian clam is hermaphroditic, it only takes one individual to slip through to start an invasion.

Following Minnesota's lead, the Ontario Federation of Anglers and Hunters (OFHA) has begun to work with the provincial government to help stop or slow the spread of invasives such as purple loosestrife and zebra mussels. Among other things, OFHA and the province have built a permanent boat-wash station at Lake Simcoe, the province's largest inland lake, and bought two portable boat-wash stations that travel to special events, such as fishing tournaments.

---

Bait shops, which are largely unregulated, are another source of invasive species. "If you were to go out to bait shops and look at what they're selling, odds are that there are some contaminant species," says Andrew R. Mahon, a molecular ecologist at Central Michigan University's Institute for Great Lakes Research. Mahon coauthored a 2012–13 study with his colleague Chris Jerde of the University of Nevada, Reno, and graduate student Lucas Nathan that demonstrated without question that the largely unregulated

An employee of the Illinois Department of Natural Resources decontaminates a state-owned boat with hot water and bleach after it is removed from Lake Michigan. Decontamination decreases the chances that the boat will transport an invasive species to another location.

bait trade is a potential pathway for exotic species.[2] Nathan spent two years collecting 576 water samples from 525 bait shops as part of a Great Lakes Restoration Initiative project to help develop genetic surveillance monitoring in the commercial bait trade in the Great Lakes basin. Using a technique that detects an animal's DNA, Nathan found six different species of invasive fish, including silver carp DNA, in the water samples. It's entirely possible that there might be a juvenile invasive carp in the bait because a juvenile silver or bighead carp looks very much like a gizzard shad sold as bait. Even though the study was looking primarily for carp DNA, Nathan found round goby, tubenose goby, and goldfish DNA in bait for sale.

It's bad enough, Mahon says, that the bait may unknowingly be contaminated, but anglers' behavior compounds the problem. "What do we all do with our bait when we are done with it? We dump it in the water," Mahon says. "You don't want to see your fish flopping around on the shore, so you dump it in the water. I know I did that as a kid."

In an attempt to make anglers aware of the risks, Sea Grant organizations are now encouraging anglers across the Great Lakes basin to bag up their unused bait and put it in trash cans. It's part of an effort by Sea Grant to educate anglers and bait dealers on live-bait pathways for aquatic invasives. Unfortunately, their efforts haven't been greeted with universal warmth, and posters and handouts have a way of disappearing after Sea Grant employees leave.

Because of fears that invasive species may be spreading through the bait trade, Credit Valley Conservation, an Ontario-based conservation authority that runs several parks northwest of Toronto, banned the importation of baitfish into the region after a round goby was found in a pond in the town of Hillsburgh. "It isn't so much the baitfish themselves that we're concerned about," says Jon Clayton, an aquatic biologist with Credit Valley Conservation. "It's other stuff that might come in with the baitfish."[3]

Clayton and other biologists are fighting an uphill battle because for years, bait-bucket biologists have been adding fish to lakes and ponds and even built up rainwater in isolated gravel pits so they can have their own private fishing holes or bait supply, according to Dan O'Keefe, an extension educator with Michigan Sea Grant. Even though people often think they're doing something innocent, the impact can be significant.

Nick Phelps, an aquaculture specialist with the University of Minnesota Extension in St. Paul, Minnesota, says it is impossible to know if the bait industry is responsible for the introduction of any exotic species. Nevertheless, he believes bait could be responsible for the introduction of viral hemorrhagic septicemia, more commonly known as VHS, a virus that causes fish to bleed to death. He believes bait is also responsible for the introduction of the Heterosporis parasite that liquefies fish muscles. The spread of VHS through contaminated bait has become so much of a concern in Ontario that the province has been forced to put some lakes under quarantine, which means that no one can transport fish caught in those lakes out of the area.

In Ontario, about twelve hundred retail outlets sell bait to about 1.3 million anglers annually. Both dealers and bait buyers often buy their bait in one location and then travel several miles to fish, which has contributed to the fast spread of VHS. Bait dealers near Lake Nipissing in Ontario often wonder how some dealers have emerald shiners to sell during the winter when their source for the fish, Lake Simcoe, is frozen over. Both bait dealers and conservation officers suspect that many of the emerald shiners coming into the area are coming from Lake Erie, which is under quarantine for VHS. Even though the province has instituted an inspection program for baitfish coming into the area, it's clear that uninspected fish are slipping through.

To stop the spread of both invasives and the virus, provincial conservation officers now require dealers to keep logs of where and how they get their bait.

During an inspection, conservation officers look for fish that are swimming in an unusual pattern that may indicate illness or fish with unusual colors or shapes that may indicate an exotic. In 2012, the first year of the inspection program, conservation officers found 153 violations in 184 visits. Even though there were 164 nonbait organisms detected, it's not as bad as it sounds; the vast majority of the violations were paperwork offenses.

———

To prevent invasives from becoming established in the Great Lakes, you first have to find them. That's the job of Stephen Hensler and Eric Stadig, who are both fish biologists with the US Fish and Wildlife Service. Hensler and Stadig are the night watchmen of the Great Lakes because it's their job to work all night from May through October, sampling water in Lake Erie's Maumee and Sandusky Bays in search of invasive species.

Hensler and Stadig are assigned to the Alpena Fish and Wildlife Conservation Office (FWCO) and are working with other FWCO biologists assigned to other Great Lakes harbors and rivers to design a program that can detect any new species in the lake. In Maumee Bay, they focus on fish, amphipods, and bivalves (mussels and clams); organisms from those three groups are likely to have a high impact if introduced to the Great Lakes. The goal of this research is to detect any new species early enough to control, prevent the spread, or even eradicate it while the population is still small. And therein is the invasive-species Catch-22: when the population is still small enough to eradicate, an individual organism is extremely difficult to detect. However, the simple discovery of a new species can help to determine the pathway into the Great Lakes, and determining that entry point can help policy makers decide what to do next. Hensler and Stadig work nights because small fish and the plankton they eat come to the surface to feed because they are less vulnerable to predators in the dark. On this particular night in early May, they plan to work Maumee Bay in western Lake Erie, just north of Toledo, Ohio.

It's easy to understand why this area is a potential hotspot for invasive-species introduction. Toledo is one of the busiest ports on the Great Lakes, with both lakers and international ships coming and going from the time the ice melts in the spring through December. Even though the international ships exchanged their ballast in the Atlantic Ocean before entering the St. Lawrence Seaway, it's still possible that they could discharge new organisms with their ballast water in Toledo. And it's possible that one or more of the four species of Asian carps could be here, introduced through the bait trade, from nearby agricultural ponds, or because they crossed from the Wabash

River watershed into the Maumee River watershed during a flood that connected the two rivers.

Hensler and Stadig plan to motor to a series of preset locations. At each location, they will trail a pair of extremely fine, five-hundred-micron nets behind their boat and slowly drive in a circle. After completing several circles, the nets will be brought onboard and the organisms collected. The contents of each net will then be placed in separate jars and labeled with time, date, and location. One jar will be sent to the US Environmental Protection Agency (EPA) laboratory in Cincinnati, Ohio, for analysis. The other half of the paired sample will be saved with plankton being frozen and larval fish being preserved in ethanol in the event a second test becomes necessary.

This type of DNA testing is called quantitative real-time polymerase chain reaction, or qPCR, and is different from the test used by Nathan, the Central Michigan University graduate student. That type of test, known as eDNA, has been in the news over the past couple of years because researchers have used it to search the Great Lakes and their tributaries for evidence of invasive grass, bighead, and silver carps. The eDNA test looks for a specific DNA marker and searches a water sample for a match. This test has found evidence of Asian carps above the electric barrier on the Chicago Sanitary and Ship Canal, in the Kalamazoo River in southwestern Michigan, and in the Lower Fox River in Wisconsin.

The qPCR test used by FWS, however, doesn't just look for a specific match. Instead, qPCR processes all the DNA found in a sample and identifies everything it finds. It's a great test for this type of sampling, but there's one major drawback: it's not as sensitive as the eDNA test, so if only a tiny amount of DNA is present in the sample, the machine that performs the sequencing may not detect it. Biologists already have the DNA of Lake Erie's native organisms and known exotics, so any new and unusual DNA will be obvious.

Summer is the best time to be on the lookout for Asian carps and many other fish species as they are all more likely to be caught when they are larvae. Therefore, the two biologists collect larval fish samples four nights a week from late spring through July.

On this particular night, however, things don't look promising. Radar shows rain and embedded thunderstorms off to the southwest, and the water temperature is still a chilly fifty-seven degrees. Rain won't stop the data collection, but other conditions—heavy winds and thunderstorms—will. Safety is a high priority, especially since they are working at night.

There's still a glow in the western sky when Hensler and Stadig leave the dock a few minutes before nine p.m. After about fifteen minutes of motoring up the river, however, it becomes apparent that this night is going to be a bust; a brisk northwesterly wind has kicked up the lake, and every time the boat hits a wave, a gusher of spray comes over the bow. Both biologists conclude that with a combination of the wind and waves and the threat of thunderstorms looming, it is just not safe out here tonight.

The night will not be a total bust, however. Both biologists plan to stay up all night, entering data, reading manuscripts, and prepping for presentations in their motel room. They will then sleep all day with the goal of being out there again the following night.

---

If it seems Hensler and Stadig are looking for a needle in a haystack, they're not. They have a firm idea of where to search for invasive species because of modeling done by the EPA in 2011 that identified high-risk locations based on shipping patterns. To create the model—known with affection as Genetic Algorithm for Rule-Set Production (GARP)—researchers identified the ports visited by each ship before entering the Great Lakes and the likely organisms in the ballast tank from each of those ports. They then tracked the ships around the Great Lakes and measured the amount of ballast water they released into each port visited.

The GARP report identified Toledo as being among the Great Lakes ports that received the most ballast-water discharges from international shipping, along with Duluth, Minnesota; Ashtabula and Sandusky, Ohio; and Gary, Indiana. Michigan has no high-risk ports; international shipping through Michigan ports has fallen way off since 2007 because of a law that requires all ballast water be treated prior to discharge. That law remains in effect despite calls from the shipping business and members of the legislature to repeal it.

Models like GARP have become important new tools in invasive-species control. Rather than waiting for invasives to arrive and measuring their impacts, researchers have gathered data to predict which species are likely to arrive, where they're likely to be found, and what the likely impact will be both economically and environmentally.

---

Reuben Keller, an environmental science professor with the Institute of Environmental Sustainability at Loyola University Chicago, has developed risk-assessment tools that will predict which species are most likely to become invasive if they are introduced, particularly those that could be introduced to the Great Lakes through the aquarium trade. Keller built a matrix for all of the fishes, mollusks, crayfish, plants, amphibians, and reptiles previously introduced to the Great Lakes. On each row of the matrix, he put a species, and on each column, he put a trait—size, diet, history of invasion in other locations, and so on. By analyzing these matrices, he was able to determine which traits make a species more likely to become established and invasive. Then, he could use these traits to drill down and predict which new species are likely to become harmful and which ones are likely to be benign.

Keller's work found specific traits—an edge over native species—that would allow invaders to dominate a niche or an entire ecosystem. He discovered that that specific trait was consistent within groups (e.g., fishes, mollusks, plants) but varied widely among groups. With fish, for example, the single most important trait in determining whether a species would become established is climate. With mollusks, however, the single most important trait is their prolific reproduction.

Overall, Keller says that of the 826 fish species in commerce that were entered into the matrix, only seven were predicted to become established, and only four of those were predicted to have a high impact on the Great Lakes. That small number, he says, is a reflection of how the aquarium trade is dominated by tropical fish that are unlikely to become established in a temperate climate.

Matching the species to the risk is the easy part. The hard part is assigning a potential economic impact because it's difficult to link the impact of a single species to a specific amount. For example, the primary ecological damage of the round goby is that it eats the eggs of desirable native fish species such as bass. The problem is it's impossible to determine an actual cost because it's impossible to know just how many bass eggs the gobies are eating and what impact they are having on bass populations.

Nevertheless, it is possible to measure the economic impact of some invasive species like the sea lamprey, because we know what governments spend on sea lamprey control. "We now spend $20 million a year on trying to kill them. If we weren't controlling them, it would cost far, far more than that," Keller says.

Still, any risk assessment or any effort to assign a number to economic impact is worthless if the federal governments and the Great Lakes states and provinces fail to work in unison to enact regulation. "A smattering of regulations across the region just isn't good enough," Keller says. "Efforts to prevent introduction are only as good as the least effective regulation. Coordination is essential."

———

The desire to have region-wide coordination recently led several state legislatures in the western United States to approve similar bills that authorize law-enforcement officers in those states to inspect watercraft when they travel across state lines. With zebra mussels spreading rapidly and water being a premium commodity in that region, those states are moving rapidly to prevent mussel movements.

Minnesota and Wisconsin have similar laws that provide for watercraft inspections at boat-launching sites. Both states require boat owners to drain their live wells and inspect their boats and trailers and remove any organisms they might find. Both states also prohibit the dumping of unused bait in a body of water; all unused bait must be put in plastic bags and then put in the trash. Minnesota, however, takes it two steps further. First, it requires all boats to be transported with their drain plugs removed or face a $100 fine. Second, the state now uses mussel-sniffing dogs to inspect watercraft to determine if the boat or trailer could be transporting zebra or quagga mussels. Anyone ticketed for unlawfully possessing or transporting a quagga or zebra mussel will face a $500 fine.

————

Unlike Minnesota, Wisconsin, and the western states, Michigan has no watercraft-inspection program. Instead, Michigan relies on the voluntary compliance of boaters who often don't know how to deal with potential invasives or just don't care. So it should come as no surprise that some of the state's most valuable bodies of water are being overrun by Eurasian watermilfoil.

One of those places is the Les Cheneaux Islands in Lake Huron near the eastern tip of Michigan's Upper Peninsula. The thirty-six islands that make up the archipelago are a summer vacation paradise. The islands and Upper Peninsula shoreline are lined with everything from million-dollar homes to at least one small shack purchased from the Sears-Roebuck catalogue more than seventy years ago. Each year, the town of Hessel hosts one of the largest shows for antique wooden boats in the country. The narrow channels and shallow bays between the islands provide some of the best swimming, boating, and fishing in the Great Lakes. In fact, it's estimated that 40 percent of the jobs in the region are tourism related.

But the shallow bays that make the fishing so spectacular also provide a place for Eurasian watermilfoil to grow. And grow. And grow.

The first patch of Eurasian watermilfoil was discovered in Cedarville Bay in 2002. On the basis of growth patterns, the Michigan Department of Environmental Quality determined that the Eurasian watermilfoil entered the area on a boat or trailer because it was first found growing near launch ramps. The milfoil spread quickly over the course of the next four summers, and low water levels meant the plant could thrive in more places. By 2006, Cedarville

Bay was so clogged with Eurasian watermilfoil that residents say a mallard duck could have walked from shoreline to shoreline.

Economically, ecologically, and psychologically, the Les Cheneaux Islands were under attack.

Ryan Thum, a former professor of molecular biology at Grand Valley State University who is now at Montana State University, has studied the genetics of Eurasian watermilfoil, but he's also seen firsthand the impacts that the plant has on recreation, boating, fishing, and swimming. Ecologically, Thum says, Eurasian watermilfoil has a big impact on a lake's physical structure because it takes over the entire nearshore area, restricting water movement, increasing sediments, and ultimately decreasing the amount of oxygen in the water. Economically, it hurts property values and burns out boat motors.

But, Thum says, it's the psychological impact of Eurasian watermilfoil that might be the biggest. People just don't like it. "They're afraid of it," Thum says. "They don't care, they just want to get rid of it. What everybody agrees on is it would be better if this thing wasn't right here."

———

Bob Smith wishes the milfoil were gone, too, and he has committed himself to making it happen. Standing on the deck of his boat, the *Grey Goose*, he squints as he looks at Sheppard Bay, one of the largest bodies of water in the Les Cheneaux Islands, and remembers how difficult it was to boat through here when the milfoil was at its peak. "We were in deep yogurt," he says.

Smith is a retired microbiologist from Abbot Laboratories in the Chicago area. Both he and his wife grew up in the eastern Upper Peninsula, and when they retired, they imagined returning here to a life of fishing, boating, and gardening. Instead, like the bays and waterways he so loves, he became consumed by milfoil. Knowing that he had important knowledge to contribute, Smith began to work with area residents and businesses to develop a Eurasian watermilfoil control strategy.

The control of aquatic invasive plants is, by its nature, difficult, Smith says. Biologists have a full toolbox when it comes to controlling terrestrial plants. They can choose from multiple chemicals, biologics, and types of applications. They can pull, mow, or burn plants or use a combination of these methods. When it comes to managing aquatic plants like Eurasian watermilfoil and hydrilla, the options are far more limited.

In other locations, chemical control likely would have been the first choice; but these are the Les Cheneaux Islands, and residents quickly rejected it because they did not want risk harming the area's fishery or turning the lake into a moonscape. Mechanical harvesting was viewed as an option, and

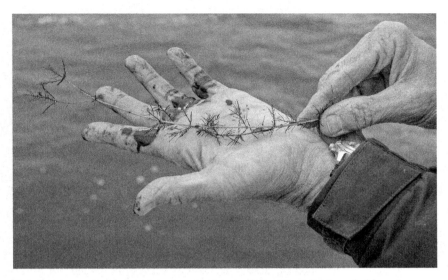

Bob Smith, a retired microbiologist who lives in Cedarville, Michigan, holds a piece of Eurasian watermilfoil, an invasive plant that now grows densely in Cedarville Bay. Smith has been working to develop a fungus that has the potential to control the plant.

the owner of a marina even bought a harvesting machine to open a pathway between his docks and the lake; but harvesting has significant disadvantages. First and foremost, it's only a temporary fix because the machine only cuts the plants and does not kill them. Second, the harvester is slow, so it's not possible to quickly clear a large area. Finally, with any kind of mechanical harvesting, there is the risk of spreading the cut milfoil to new areas.

Given the limitations, area residents, the local watershed council, and state and local governments decided it was worth taking a chance on something new and different. It was time to release the weevils. A weevil is a tiny beetle that is best known as an agricultural pest that damages crops. Of course, the best-known member of the family is the boll weevil that infested and wiped out the cotton crop in the southern United States in the 1920s. Was it possible that its northern water-loving cousin could be sicced on an invasive plant?

In 2007, after receiving permission from the EPA and the Michigan Department of Environmental Quality, Clark Township released fifteen thousand native aquatic weevils (*Euhrychiopsis lecontei*) on the largest patches of Eurasian watermilfoil in Cedarville Bay. Within a year, the weevils had reduced the plant by about 85 percent in treated areas.

The weevils are native to eastern and central North America and usually eat northern watermilfoil, a native plant. But they also have been found to be highly effective against the invasive milfoil. Adult weevils eat both the leaves and stem of the plant, but in the larvae stage, the weevils bore into the stem, causing damage to the plant's vascular system. Before long, the weevil has done so much damage that the plant loses buoyancy and falls over. As insects go, this weevil is unusual because it spends almost its entire life underwater.

Even though the weevil proved extremely effective at controlling milfoil, it wasn't the silver bullet local residents wanted. Weevils couldn't be applied in areas with heavy boat traffic because of the chance they would be chopped up by propellers. That drawback meant yet another solution was necessary.

This is when Bob Smith raised his hand. Smith knew that in the early 1980s, the Army Corps of Engineers, the University of Massachusetts at Amherst, the US Department of Agriculture, and the University of Florida had been studying a fungus, *Mycoleptodiscus terrestris* (Mt), to control Eurasian watermilfoil. Even though those studies showed promise, research was abandoned because the fungus was notoriously difficult to work with because it needed to be cultured differently from other biological control agents and it had a short shelf life. Smith went to work and contacted the US Department of Agriculture (USDA) laboratory in Peoria, Illinois, to learn if small amounts of the fungus could be made available for experimentation with the milfoil. Using Mt produced in Peoria, Smith ran multiple successful trials that showed the fungus effectively controlled the milfoil under a wide range of conditions. Despite the tender loving care it takes to culture Mt, Smith says it's worth the effort because it's safe and effective and doesn't have any of the drawbacks of the herbicides.

Smith and a project team have developed field data and proof that Mt can effectively manage Eurasian watermilfoil sufficient to justify development of a commercial product. He says he doesn't have the desire to run a business these days but will help transition Mt from the field-trial stage to commercial scale with a third-party manufacturer. So when Mt is finally produced commercially, Smith intends for all the profits to go to the company that makes it, and negotiated royalties will be shared between the Les Cheneaux Watershed Council and the USDA lab in Peoria, rather than going to Smith personally.

So, is this fungus a solution that can be taken nationwide? "You bet," Smith says. "Absolutely. There's no reason this can't be produced in large quantities and shipped around the country. For inland lakes, something like this is very badly needed."

Smith thinks the fungus could come to market in just a few years and thinks regulatory approval will be streamlined since much of the preregulatory work has already been done by the Army Corps of Engineers and USDA.

———

The lessons from Lake Manitou and the Les Cheneaux Islands are obvious. First, it's possible to control and even in some circumstances to eradicate hydrilla and Eurasian watermilfoil. Second, preventing the spread of invasive species is far more cost-effective than having to deal with them once they are established. Third, control is an ongoing endeavor because even though it appears that hydrilla has been eliminated from Lake Manitou, the Indiana DNR is compelled to monitor other lakes and ponds in northern Indiana for years to come—just in case.

"This is money well spent," Fischer says. "If we had not done anything, this would have spread. We spent the money and got the result we were looking for. . . . Hydrilla certainly would have been in the Great Lakes if we had not taken action."

The Indiana DNR gets credit for doing everything it could to prevent the spread of hydrilla because it was in its best interest. But now Indiana and the other Great Lakes states are facing an even bigger challenge from two species that have the potential to wipe out what's left of the Great Lakes food web. The question is, will states do everything they can to prevent these species from spreading when there are competing interests?

# 7

# THE LURKING THREAT

It's not easy to get around Eagle Marsh Nature Preserve in southwestern Fort Wayne, Indiana. It's wet and muddy in lots of places—it is a marsh, after all. But Betsy Yankowiak, the director of preserves and programs for the Little River Wetlands Project, the nonprofit that administers the marsh, can take you where you need to go.

Hop in a John Deere Gator Utility Vehicle, and she'll drive until you get to a spot where the water is so deep it's impassable. From there, scramble up a canary-grass-covered berm and try to keep up with Yankowiak on a five-minute walk until you see the Asian carps fence.

It's a cyclone fence, more than seventeen hundred feet long and eight feet high. Its bottom is anchored two feet into the ground, and the posts are supported by concrete Jersey barriers. The fence runs in a zigzag between the berm and a busy railroad grade on the south, and it cost about $200,000, paid for with federal dollars from the Great Lakes Restoration Initiative.

This fence is here, Yankowiak explains, because this marsh is a low spot in the continental divide that separates the Mississippi River basin from the Great Lakes. There are many potential pathways for the invasive Asian carps in the Mississippi River to spread into the Great Lakes, and this marsh is one of them.

Asian carps—bighead, silver, grass, and black—may be the most widely feared and misunderstood invasive species in North America. Two of the four—silver and bighead—have made their way up the Mississippi River and into several tributaries. One of those tributaries, the Illinois River, connects directly to Lake Michigan.

Compared to the bighead and silver carp, the black carp has a relatively tiny population, but black carps have been steadily moving up the

107

Mississippi River too and are now in the lower Illinois River. Meanwhile, it's feared that the grass carp—considered by some biologists to be less destructive—is already in the Great Lakes, specifically, Lake Erie. A breeding population of grass carps was found in the Sandusky River in Ohio in 2012.

Those Sandusky River grass carps may not be the only ones in the Great Lakes. Between 2011 and 2014, commercial fishing operations based in Monroe County, Michigan, caught twenty-four grass carps in the lake's western basin. Laboratory tests found that some of those carp were sterile but that others were fertile. With so many carp being caught, biologists knew they had a problem but one that was limited to the western basin on Lake Erie. Or so they thought.

In July 2015 biologists caught a grass carp during a wetland restoration project on an island in Lake Ontario just off the shore of downtown Toronto. The next day, they caught a second one in a nearby pond.

Both were males, and both were fertile.

Over the course of the summer, four more grass carps were caught in or near Lake Ontario; two were caught in Canadian waters of Lake Erie and one was found dead in the lower Niagara River. It's not the numbers that were most troubling; it was that six of nine carp caught were fertile—including one female. Before then, only three grass carps had been caught in Canadian waters, and all were sterile.

The discoveries—particularly of the fertile fish—left Canadian officials mystified but determined to find answers. How old were the fish? Where did they come from and how did they get here? Could they have been intentionally released in those island ponds? Could they have escaped from the same pond in the United States and ended up in the same area on the other side of the lake?

Becky Cudmore, the Asian carp program manager and senior researcher at Fisheries and Oceans Canada, and other Canadian biologists are starting to put pieces of the puzzle together. Besides analyzing tissue in her own lab in Burlington, Cudmore sent parts of the carp to labs at Bowling Green State University, University of Windsor, and USGS to determine age and origin.

Even though Cudmore has more questions than answers, she does know two things for certain. First, the two fish caught in July did not originate in Lake Ontario. The odolith—the tiny bone in a fish's ear—can be chemically analyzed to determine where a fish has been based on its chemical structure. An oxygen isotope analysis on the two males caught in July showed that the fish originated at a fish farm in the United States. That said, it is impossible to know which fish farm exactly, which makes

Lindsay Chadderton, the aquatic-invasive-species director for the Nature Conservancy's Great Lakes Project, collects water samples from Lake Michigan near Chicago, Illinois. Chadderton is part of a monitoring effort that is searching for the DNA of Asian carps. Although the carps have not been found in Lake Michigan, their eDNA has been found in the Chicago River near where the lake flows into the river. Photo © Paul Merideth.

it far more difficult to trace their movements. Second, it's unlikely the fish spawned because the ponds did not have the correct conditions and it appears they lacked any potential mates.

Although Cudmore is determined to find out as much as she can about these carp, chemical analysis can only provide so much information and it appears likely she will never have the answer to the ultimate question: How did they get here?

It looks bleak for preventing the establishment of the grass carp in Lake Erie, but it's not too late to prevent the further spread of the bighead and silver carps. Those two carps are most feared by biologists because they are the ones capable of doing the most damage if they were able to reach the Great Lakes. That is why some form of prevention at Eagle Marsh was so important. The wetland separates the Wabash River watershed on the west and the Maumee River watershed, which flows to Lake Erie, on the east. Even though this area is similar to a continental divide, it's not exactly the spine of the Rocky Mountains, as there is no obvious demarcation. Asked about where one watershed ends and the other begins, Yankowiak jokes, "We just crossed it. Didn't you feel it?"

The closest known population of bighead and silver carps is in the Wabash River, seventeen miles away. For one of those carps to cross from one watershed to the other, it would have to swim from the Wabash into the Little River, then into Graham McCulloch Ditch, and hit it during one of the occasional floods that temporarily unites the two watersheds. If the carp makes it across the watershed divide, it could swim into Junk Ditch, which flows into the St. Marys River, which flows into the Maumee River, which flows into Lake Erie.

There is no evidence, Yankowiak says, that there are invasive carps in the Little River or Graham McCulloch Ditch. She says the US Geological Survey has placed acoustic tags in a handful of carps in the Wabash River and has installed listening devices in the Little River, and so far none of the tagged fish has passed any of the listening devices. But that did not stop policy makers from installing a fence full of holes. It might prevent adult carps from swimming through, but it would do nothing to stop the small juveniles.

Like so many invasive-species measures, the fence is here because it was a political solution. Policy makers on both the state and federal levels felt they needed to do something—they needed to show they were taking action to reduce risk. Like many political solutions, a carp fence was both temporary and ridiculous.

In 2015, the fence was replaced with a ten-foot-high, eighty-foot-wide earthen berm, built to permanently separate the two basins, at a cost of $2.2 million. But even the more permanent berm seems like a waste of time and money when there's a direct waterway between the carps in the Illinois River and the Great Lakes, and there is no sign that it will be closed anytime soon.

––––––––

Bighead, silver, grass, and black carps are all native to China. All four carp species have been grown in Chinese aquaculture for more than one thousand years and have been a major source of food in China for centuries. Grass carps (*Ctenopharyngodon idella*) were brought to the United States in 1963 by the FWS. Some fish were given to Auburn University, and the college imported additional grass carps in 1964 and 1965 to investigate their ability to control aquatic plants in aquaculture and agricultural ponds.[1] It's clear that both the university and state governments in the US South saw potential for this usage because by 1974 there were more than 380,000 grass carps stocked into more than one hundred public or semipublic lakes in Arkansas alone.

Bighead (*Hypophthalmichthys nobilis*) and silver carps (*Hypophthalmichthys molitrix*) were brought to the United States by Jim Malone, an Arkansas fish farmer, in 1973.[2] Malone did not keep the fish, however. In 1974, he transferred the carps to the Arkansas Game and Fish Commission to see if the agency could get the fish to spawn.[3]

As surprising as it seems today, Malone imported the two carp species with the federal government's blessing. At the time, the fish were viewed as a beneficial, natural, and environmentally friendly way to control excessive plankton growth in wastewater treatment and agricultural ponds. Waterways in the US South were highly polluted by raw sewage because most small communities were too poor to afford treatment systems. Fish could be placed in the waterways and sewage ponds to eat wastes and the plankton that grew in those wastes, and then the fish could be harvested and eaten.

Black carps (*Mylopharyngodon piceus*) were first brought to North America by accident in the early 1970s—a "contaminant" in a shipment of grass carps.[4] In the 1980s, however, black carps were intentionally imported for human consumption and as a means of controlling snails and yellow grubs (a parasitic fluke) in aquaculture ponds.

Popular belief is that the grass, bighead, and silver carps escaped into the Mississippi River system in the 1970s or 1980s when Arkansas aquaculture facilities flooded. But a paper presented at a 2011 American Fisheries Society symposium laid the blame squarely at the feet of the US federal government: "The first known accidental release of diploid (fertile) grass carp was in 1966 by the U.S. Fish and Wildlife Service in Stuttgart, Arkansas. Other early reports of grass carp were from waters in Alabama, Georgia, and Florida.

Grass carp were reported in the wild in 1970, 2 years before the first private hatchery received grass carp."[5]

The paper goes on to say that the first confirmed silver carp in the wild was discovered in 1975 in Arkansas, which was two years before bighead and silver carps were sent to private hatcheries for commercial production. It's easy to be suspicious of the paper's motivations given that the majority of the authors represent the aquaculture industry, but among the authors is Andrew J. Mitchell, a retired employee of the Stuttgart National Aquaculture Research Center, which is a US Department of Agriculture facility in Arkansas. Still, the report concedes that major floods allowed additional carps to escape from southern fish farms.

Since the bighead and silver carps established themselves in southern waterways, they have been steadily spreading, following the Mississippi River as far south as Louisiana and as far north as Minnesota. They can also be found in the Missouri River as far west as South Dakota and in the Ohio River as far east as Pennsylvania.

How the black carp entered the wild is also a matter of debate. The US Geological Survey (USGS) purports that thirty or more black carps along with several thousand bighead carps escaped into the Osage River when a Missouri fish farm flooded in 1994. The owners of the Missouri facility, however, deny that any escaped. The USGS also asserts that hundreds of young black carps were accidentally included in shipments of live bait that was sent to Missouri from Arkansas starting in 1994. Some of those carps likely ended up in the wild.

Debate as we might the carps' introductions, the reality is that they're here, they're doing considerable damage to ecosystems, and biologists say it's time to finally deal with them because the future of the Great Lakes is at risk.

Once bighead and silver carps enter an ecosystem, they can dominate and decimate. In some rivers, there are places where the two species now make up more than 90 percent of fish biomass, much to the detriment of native paddlefish, shovelnose sturgeon, catfish, buffaloes, freshwater drums, and redhorses. If bighead and silver carps were to enter the Great Lakes, the yellow perch and walleye—two popular sport fish—would likely be among the first native fish species affected, according to Jim Bredin, the former associate director and deputy director for Asian carps in the White House Council on Environmental Quality.[6]

Most people are familiar with silver carps because of the YouTube videos that show them jumping out of the water at the approach of a motorboat. (Because of that, the silver carp is incorrectly synonymous with "Asian carp.") In the videos, carps are seen jumping into boats, breaking boaters' noses, knocking them over, or just knocking them cold.

Silver carps pack a wallop, too. They can grow as large as three feet and weigh as much as sixty pounds. Adult bighead carps, meanwhile, average between twenty-four and thirty-six inches long and weigh in the neighborhood of forty pounds, but they can get bigger. One bow hunter on the Mississippi River caught a bighead carp that weighed ninety-two pounds.

The carps were present in the Illinois River in small numbers in the late 1990s, but the population took off about the year 2000. It's impossible to know just how many fish are in the river at any one time, but there have been years when commercial fishers have removed more than one hundred thousand individuals.

Bighead and silver carps in their native range in Asia have exacting requirements for spawning: they need a large, unimpeded river at least sixty miles long. During a flood or high water, the fish swim up the river, breed, and let the high water carry the incubating eggs back down to a wetland at the mouth of the tributary. The eggs have to remain buoyant for up to thirty hours to hatch and will die if they settle in an oxygen-poor portion of the river.

In North America, however, bighead and silver carps have surprised researchers by their incredible ability to adapt:

- They can spawn in shorter rivers, possibly as short as nine miles.

- They are able to spawn in narrower rivers with lower discharge rates than their cousins back in their native range.

- Incubation time for the eggs has fallen by four to six hours.

- In North America, the fish have a longer spawning season.

- In Asia, the fish spawn once a year. In North America, they have confounded biologists by spawning three times in some years and not at all in others.

Female bighead carps can produce as many as 872,000 eggs a year, and a single female silver carp can produce as many as two million eggs a year. Grass carps, meanwhile, can grow up to fifty inches long and weigh as much as much as forty pounds, and black carps—the monster of the group—can grow as long as six feet and weigh as much as 220 pounds. Female grass carps produce as many as a million eggs a year, while black carps can produce as many as 1.8 million eggs a year. Given the size and fast growth rate of these fish, they have few predators.

They're not just big and prolific. They're smart, too. Commercial fishermen say that the carps have learned to identify and avoid nets, which makes them very difficult to catch. They're also voracious. All four carp species would do well in a competitive eating contest. Bighead and silver carps are filter feeders; silver carps primarily consume phytoplankton, while bighead carps eat phytoplankton, zooplankton, and detritus, including zebra and quagga pseudofeces. The two species have adaptations that make them extremely efficient feeders—they suck in food and strain it to concentrate it in their mouths, then excrete excess water through their gills. Both species can consume up to 20 percent of their body weight in a day. Because both species consume so much plankton, they are in direct competition with native mussels and other fish that feed on plankton.

Bighead and silver carps have had a profound influence on the food web in the Illinois River. A 2014 study compared the current composition and abundance in the zooplankton community in different stretches of the Illinois River to historical records.[7] The study showed that after the carps established their population, the abundance of zooplankton and phytoplankton decreased significantly, leaving less food for native mussels and juvenile fish.

Ordinarily an invasive like these carps would have eaten themselves into equilibrium with the available plankton. But a USGS study has shown that when plankton is scarce, the fish will shift their diets to consume the organic matter on the river bottom—fish poop—and bacteria.

Black carps, meanwhile, feast on as much as four pounds of mollusks a day. Adult grass carps can eat as much as 40 percent of their body weight in a day, but juvenile grass carps are a lot like teenage boys in that they are nonstop eating machines. Young carps that weigh around two and a half pounds can eat as much as three hundred times their body weight in a day. In fact, grass carps are so voracious that many northern states banned them out of fear that they would devastate native aquatic vegetation.

Biologists also fear the carps will make Lake Erie's now-regular blooms of cyanobacteria even worse. For the past decade, the lake has been suffering from the effects of massive blooms of cyanobacteria, specifically microcystis, a photosynthetic bacterium that produces the toxin microcystin. The toxin, which can cause liver damage and even death in humans, was responsible for making the water undrinkable for the city of Toledo, Ohio, and a small part of southeastern Michigan in early August 2014. A simple solution might seem to be allowing sterile silver carps loose to cruise around western Lake Erie to consume massive amounts of the algae. But a USGS study found that certain types of cyanobacteria enhance their toxin production in response to the presence of the carps. Even though the toxin will not kill the fish, it will accumulate in the fish's body, potentially in high enough amounts to be fatal to any mammal that eats it.

Becky Cudmore of Fisheries and Oceans Canada says that when you combine the carps' fast growth rate with their astounding ability to reproduce and voracious appetites, you have a group of invaders that must be prevented from spreading into the Great Lakes. Dan O'Keefe of Michigan Sea Grant agrees and adds that the carps are incredibly adaptable to conditions, which also helps to make them so invasive.

Even though the carps have shown they're smart and adaptable, they are surprisingly fragile, says Robin Calfee, a biologist with the USGS in Columbia, Missouri. If a carp scrapes against a rough surface, it will expose raw tissue. Within a few days, a fungus can grow on the raw tissue that will eventually kill the fish. The carps' backbones are surprisingly fragile, too. Crews conducting electrofishing surveys have discovered that the current from electrodes in the water is enough to blow out a carp's spine.

Nevertheless, biologists believe that if the silver and bighead carps make it into the Great Lakes, they will decimate what's left of a $7 billion commercial fishing industry and sport fishery by occupying tributaries and consuming the plankton that feed the small native fish.

Some scientists believe, however, that the threat to Lake Michigan is overblown. John Janssen, a professor in the School of Freshwater Sciences at the University of Wisconsin–Milwaukee, says the bighead and silver carps can't do much more damage to Lake Michigan than what has already been done. "There's virtually no phytoplankton in Lake Michigan left to sustain the Asian carp," Janssen told a Milwaukee public radio station in 2013.[8] On the other hand, Janssen worries about what might happen if the carp were to reach Lake Erie, which is a far more productive lake because of the influx of nutrients.

To stop the spread of the bighead, silver, and black carps in particular, the US and Canadian governments and the Great Lakes states have begun to coordinate and are now devoting considerable resources to their efforts. On the Canadian side, where only an occasional grass carp is found, efforts have focused on risk assessment, early detection and monitoring, and just-in-case preparation. In the United States, both federal and state agencies have been cooperating to create a comprehensive strategy—when they're not fighting among themselves.

In 2010, US President Barack Obama appointed John Goss, the former executive director of the Indiana Wildlife Federation, as the chairman of the new Asian Carp Regional Coordinating Committee (ACRCC). Since then, the ACRCC has been developing policies to monitor carp movements and trap and remove carps that are outlined in the group's 2013 Asian Carp Monitoring and Response Plan (MRP). The MRP creates a framework for

$6.5 million of monitoring, sampling, and response activities to be conducted by a combination of state and federal agencies.

In 2012, the Army Corps released a study that identified eighteen possible pathways for the carps to reach the Great Lakes, ranging from New York State on the east to Minnesota on the west. After identifying the pathways, the Corps assigned a level of risk to each. Ten were assessed as low risk, and seven were viewed as medium risk. Only one pathway was viewed as a high risk: the Chicago Area Waterway System.

The Chicago Area Waterway System, or CAWS, is a one-hundred-mile system of rivers and canals that connects the Mississippi tributaries to the Great Lakes through five access points to Lake Michigan, with one branch running south to meet the Calumet River and reaching as far east as Burns Harbor, Indiana, and another running north to Wilmette, Illinois. The main artery is the Chicago Sanitary and Ship Canal (CSSC), which connects to Lake Michigan through the Chicago River in downtown Chicago. The CSSC is an engineering marvel that allows barges and pleasure craft to travel from Lake Michigan to the Mississippi River and eventually to New Orleans and the Gulf of Mexico.

The canal was completed in 1900 because the Chicago River at that time was a little more than an open sewer, carrying human waste and other untreated runoff from the city into Lake Michigan, which was also the source of the city's drinking water. To protect the city's drinking water, city leaders in 1887 decided to build a canal that would send the city's wastewater west, to the Des Plaines River, the Illinois River, and eventually into the Mississippi River north of St. Louis. The first step in the construction was to cut through a ridge twelve miles inland that separated the Great Lakes and Mississippi River watersheds. The second step was to reverse the flow of the Chicago River so that it would flow *out of* Lake Michigan to push and dilute the city's wastewater.

Despite improvements to Chicago's water-treatment system, the canal remains highly polluted, so much so that it is lined with signs warning against any human contact. Sewage from the city is treated before being pumped into the canal, but large rain events cause the system to overflow, forcing massive amounts of untreated sewage into the canal.

---

Concern over the Chicago Area Waterway System as a pathway for the spread of invasive species began after the Eurasian ruffe rapidly took over Duluth-Superior Harbor in 1986, raising concerns that the fish would quickly spread across North America. In 1996, with the passage of the National Invasive Species Act, Congress sought to pinch the flow of exotic species from the Great

Lakes into the Mississippi River and ordered the US Army Corps of Engineers to construct a demonstration barrier that would stop the passage of fish.

The Army Corps is responsible for maintaining all navigable waterways in the United States, and it became the job of Phil Moy, the Chicago District's fish biologist, to find a solution. Moy already had experience working on fish barriers, so he knew that he needed to pull together every agency he thought had regulatory authority or commercial interest in the project. He also knew that if it was exclusively a federal operation, it would never get local support, so he added stakeholders from the state and local governments and nongovernmental organizations and ended up with a fifteen-member committee.

After months of debate, the committee concluded that it could not tamper with wastewater discharge and navigation. Once the committee began to explore what type of barrier might be best to stop the fish, its members quickly agreed that they did not want to use toxins at the risk of turning vast portions of the river into a dead zone. After eliminating other barriers because the technology was in its infancy or simply wasn't good enough, the committee was left with four potential solutions: bubbles, lights, sound, and electricity. Moy says fish biologists knew that visual barriers and sound can alter the behavior of fish and change their movements, but the committee eventually agreed that an electric barrier was the best choice.

Initially, Moy says, the Corps had very little money to work with. Even though Congress authorized $500,000 a year, the project never got its full allotment—sometimes as little as half. Nevertheless, an electrical barrier was completed in 2002, but not before the round goby was able to pass from the Great Lakes into the Mississippi River basin. The Eurasian ruffe, meanwhile, has yet to establish a population anywhere in southern Lake Michigan. With the battle against the goby lost and the battle against the Eurasian ruffe still on the horizon, the focus of the demonstration barrier shifted from preventing fish from escaping the Great Lakes to preventing the spread of carps into the Great Lakes.

----

The Asian carps barrier is actually three different barriers built into the riverbed of the CSSC near Romeoville, Illinois, twenty-five miles west of Chicago. The barriers are twenty-five miles above the carps' population front in the Illinois River. No one knows why, but that population front has not moved for almost a decade. Although no one knows why the carp have not continued to move up river, Kevin Irons, the invasive species coordinator for Illinois DNR, speculates the fish simply don't like the water coming out of the CAWS. Could it be that we found a redeeming quality for raw sewage?

David Wethington, a project manager for the US Army Corps of Engineers Chicago District, says the original barrier was considered state of the art when it was constructed, but the Corps soon realized it needed redundancy since the barrier would occasionally need to be shut down for maintenance. In 2007, Congress authorized the construction of two additional barriers—Barriers 2A and 2B—and in 2013, construction was started on a permanent replacement for the original Demonstration Barrier.

The barriers produce different voltages. The Demonstration Barrier produces one volt per square inch at five hertz (which means it goes off five times per second, and each cycle lasts for four milliseconds). Barriers 2A and 2B each produce 2.3 volts per inch, but the electrodes on 2B are closer to each other, which has the effect of making the voltage more intense. It's unlikely that a large fish will make it past 2A, however, because bigger fish have more area to absorb the electric current. The voltage in 2B, meanwhile, is effective against a fish as small as two and a half inches long. Barrier 2A is designed to make a fish uncomfortable. The narrower array of electrodes on Barrier 2B is designed to incapacitate a fish. Any fish headed upriver that comes in contact with the current will be stunned, and the canal's current will push it back below Barrier 2A before it can recover.

"There's a lot of confidence that existing measures are enough," Wethington says. "If that changes, then certainly our responsibility would have to change."

The barriers are constructed in the bed of a navigable waterway, one that carries regular barge traffic and the occasional pleasure boat. Although no one has ever tested it, there is concern about what might happen to a human who falls overboard. Could the electrical current cause muscle, nerve, or heart damage? Because of that possibility, there are large signs posed on the canal to notify approaching watercraft of the hazard. And for security purposes, cameras keep tabs on the comings and goings of watercraft, and armed guards protect the facility 24/7. In addition, there are on-site generators in the event of a power outage. Today, the barriers cost about $12 million a year to operate and maintain, and each barrier uses about $60,000 a month in electricity.

The barriers, however, are far from foolproof. After the barriers were shut down for maintenance in the fall of 2009, University of Notre Dame researchers told the Corps that thirty-two water samples taken from the CSSC between the electric barriers and Lake Michigan tested positive for silver carp eDNA. In response to the positive eDNA, the Illinois Department of Natural Resources (DNR) poisoned a 5.7-mile stretch of the waterway above the Demonstration Barrier, killing thousands of fish. Among those was a single twenty-two-inch-long bighead carp.

Although there are backup generators at the site, the barriers were shut down for a thirteen-minute stretch during May 2012 because of a power failure. The backup generators kicked in immediately upon the power failure, but the power surge tripped a circuit breaker, which had to be identified and reset.

The Army Corps of Engineers maintains that the electric barriers are robust enough to protect the Great Lakes from marauding carps, but the Corps seems to be in the minority, especially after it issued a study in late 2013 that said it was possible for fish to be carried through the barriers if they passed through with a barge. The study used high-definition sonar to follow fish movements at the barriers and discovered that not only could fish make it across the barrier if they became caught up in the wake of a barge, but schools of small fish regularly made it across the barrier with no barge traffic present.

When moving raw goods in the canal, a tug usually pushes several barges of different shapes and sizes at the same time. In tracking the movements of fish, the Corps discovered that the way those differently shaped barges were arranged had a significant impact on the power of the electrical current. Some barge arrangements had the effect of significantly increasing the current measured by sensors in the water, while other barge arrangements had the effect of significantly reducing the current "to the point that it is barely measureable."[9] The report also said that the Corps would continue to study the issue in hopes it could find a solution.

The Corps' report was greeted with derision by people who are working to protect the Great Lakes. "The Corps has put so much faith in the electrical barrier, but we know that the fish can swim right through it," says Chris Jerde, a postdoctoral researcher at the University of Notre Dame's Environmental Change Initiative who is now at the University of Nevada–Reno. Jerde was among a small band of researchers who helped to pioneer the development of the eDNA screening method. Prior to the development of the eDNA technique, wildlife managers had two techniques to survey a river's fish population: pumping electricity into the water from a boat to stun the fish, or poison. Each technique has its drawbacks, but compared to shocking or poisoning a river, eDNA is far more efficient and cost-effective.

Notre Dame gets credit for pioneering the eDNA technique, but four different groups around the world were working independently on the same idea at the same time. Notre Dame's article on the eDNA technique was the first to garner attention because it dealt with a hot and controversial topic.

Among biologists and wildlife managers, the joke about eDNA is that it is like a famous Homer Simpson quote: "Here's to alcohol: the cause of, and solution to, all of life's problems." Substitute "eDNA" for "alcohol," and you get the idea; it's a tool that biologists need to use as part of any monitoring program and dread using because they fear what they might find. Even though eDNA may provide evidence, it doesn't necessarily provide you with a fish.

Environmental DNA—or eDNA for short—is the stuff that falls off an animal. It's as small as a hair, a fleck of skin, a feather, a scale, or some fish slime, and its presence indicates that an animal was *likely* in or close to that

Storing eDNA samples. Lindsay Chadderton packs two-liter plastic bottles that have been filled with water from Lake Michigan near Chicago. The water inside the bottles will be analyzed for the DNA of invasive carp species as part of a monitoring project that hopes to prevent the carps' spread into the Great Lakes. Photo © Paul Merideth.

location recently. When a human walks into a room, he or she will likely leave some eDNA behind. Of course, establishing that that particular human was indeed in the room means being lucky enough to find this tiny bit of DNA. The same is true with Asian carps.

In 2014, routine sampling in the Fox River in Wisconsin and the Kalamazoo River in Michigan, both important tributaries to Lake Michigan, turned up positive samples for invasive carps. FWS and the departments of natural resources in both Michigan and Wisconsin stepped up monitoring for weeks following the positive hits, including conducting electrofishing on long stretches of each river. No carps were discovered, and no additional positive hits were recorded.

Although the news of the carp DNA gave some Great Lakes conservation organizations the opportunity to issue alarmist press releases, Lindsay Chadderton, an aquatic-invasive-species specialist for the Nature Conservancy and a partner in Notre Dame's Environmental Change Initiative, believes we should not panic every time we get a single positive eDNA sample, as one positive hit does not make a fish. Chadderton understands that the DNA could have been transported to those rivers in multiple ways—through the guts of gulls, cormorants, or other birds or through water from a bait dealer or from a fishing boat that had recently been moved from an area where carps were present. Because of all those pathways for transport, Chadderton believes that we need to use the eDNA technology to build a case—through repeated positive hits—that demonstrates there is indeed an established population in a location before taking additional action.

Even though Chadderton counsels restraint, he's increasingly worried that we're not working quickly enough to improve our surveillance techniques. The eDNA of Asian carps has consistently been found in the North Shore Canal, the Chicago River, and the Calumet River during 2010–14. Chadderton says that even though the eDNA indicates there are fish present, specifically silver carps, crews have been unable to catch them through traditional fishing methods—electroshocking and nets that go eight feet deep in a thirty-foot deep channel. Because crews are unable to actually catch a fish in the locations of positive eDNA hits, they conclude it's a false negative—the fish must not be there.

Chadderton believes there are Asian carps in the CAWS, but they are likely there in very small numbers. Of course, that raises any number of questions:

- How many fish are there in the waterway?

- Are these the same few fish that have been there for a few years?

- Or are these new fish that have replaced the old fish that have moved someplace else?

Unfortunately, no one has yet developed surveillance techniques that can answer those questions, which means, four years later, that we are still stuck on the same question: if we have positive eDNA tests, what do they mean?

So far, there's no evidence that the small number of carps in the CAWS have found each other and have been able to find a place that is suitable for spawning. Even if the carps can find a place that's suitable for reproduction, the Chicago River and connecting waterways in the CAWS are very unlikely to provide areas where the eggs can hatch. Given all those conditions, Chadderton believes the fight to prevent the carps from leaving the Illinois River is not over yet.

Andrew Mahon, the Central Michigan University molecular ecologist and colleague of Jerde's and Chadderton's at Notre Dame, agrees that eDNA and surveillance efforts have their drawbacks but argues that it's better to get a positive hit and have no carps present than to have carps present and not know about it. No technique is perfect, and Mahon, Jerde, and Chadderton all admit that it's possible for a carp to be present in a location and still avoid detection because there's a random aspect to both the sampling and capture techniques.

In the time between a positive hit and an effort to catch the fish, it could be in a different part of the river. It's also possible for a carp to avoid eDNA detection because water samples just fail to pick up a strand of DNA. Besides, DNA is not permanent; microbes and the ultraviolet light from the sun break down eDNA in a matter of hours to days to weeks, depending on conditions.

In just a few short years, eDNA has become established as a valuable tool in early detection efforts for invasive species. Initially, however, Mahon was surprised by how much pushback he received from other biologists and wildlife managers when the technology was introduced. Some thought the science was bunk and compared it to a glorified science-fair project.

Initially, Mahon says, opponents argued that the DNA got in a certain location because it was dumped there from bait bucket, or somebody cleaned a fish there, or the DNA came out of storm sewers. "They wave their hands all around, but they have yet to show us," Mahon says. "I've learned to deal with it."

Jerde, meanwhile, has experienced the same pushback but says he's not trying to make people look good or bad. "The reputation of the Army Corps of Engineers is at stake here, because every fish found above the barrier is a hit to the agency," Jerde says. "The Corps has put so much faith in the electrical barrier, but we know that the fish can swim right through it. The barrier was turned off for a month in 2008. Anything between the two barriers could have swum right on through to the Great Lakes."

To prevent the carps from entering Lake Michigan, Jerde sees only one viable solution: permanently separate the Great Lakes from the Mississippi River. "We don't need more monitoring or electrical barriers," Jerde says. "We need action on permanent separation."

---

In January 2014, the US Army Corps of Engineers looked at stopping the flow of water from the Great Lakes to the Mississippi River by building a barrier or permanently closing locks on the CSSC as options for preventing the movement of Asian carps in its Great Lakes and Mississippi Interbasin Study (GLMRIS) on ways to prevent the spread of invasive species between watersheds.

The GLMRIS report outlined eight options, ranging from no additional controls to permanent closure of the waterway. No additional controls would obviously maintain the status quo, cost nothing more than the current amount, and take no time to complete. The eighth option, which was the most extensive and expensive, would be to build a barrier across the CSSC that makes a complete hydrological separation of the two basins. That option, the Corps said, would cost $8.3 billion and take twenty-five years to complete.

But as progress on a solution moves forward, policy makers overly concerned with carps are usually forgetting about one thing: the CAWS and the CSSC are a two-way street, and there are more—far more—types of organisms to be concerned with than just fish. In 2011, a report commissioned by the Corps identified eighty-seven species in the Great Lakes that could cross the barrier and enter the Mississippi River watershed.[10] Meanwhile, there are fifty-seven species in the Mississippi River watershed—including the Asian carps—that could cross into the Great Lakes. An electric dispersal barrier likely does nothing to stop a spiny water flea or a Japanese fish louse from moving into the Mississippi basin with the current of the river.

Now that the issue is before Congress, the question of how best to protect the Great Lakes is being discussed in a highly political arena, and decisions will be influenced by economics, inertia, lobbying, and budgets.

Start with the canal itself. More than $1.7 billion in goods pass through the CSSC every year. Most of that value comes from the shipping of coal, grain, petroleum, and chemicals. With numbers like that, you understand why the governments in Indianapolis and Springfield will fight hard in Congress to keep the waterway open.

Then look at the Corps' report itself. It's colorful and full of information and options, but it's hardly a roadmap to a solution. The first legislation said come up with two or three design options and give them to the assistant secretary of the army for civil works, who will pick one or two, says Phil Moy. "It was, 'Corps lead the way.' Instead, they [the Corps] come out with this wishy-washy, spineless report. . . . They don't make a single recommendation," Moy says. "They leave it to citizens and have them tell Congress what to do. It puts the Corps in a perfect position. They're waiting for Congress to tell them what to do," Moy says. "If it goes wrong, it's Congress's fault."

Wethington vigorously denies Moy's contention that the Corps punted on the GLMRIS report. The Corps, he says, simply complied with Congress's original authorization that asked the Corps to complete a report in eighteen months. "Control of aquatic invasive species is a shared responsibility," Wethington says. "The corps is well suited to lead, but there are many stakeholders that deserve a vote or some kind of say: the state of Illinois, the city of Chicago, water resource managers, the Metropolitan Water Reclamation District. All these stakeholders have a say. While we have made a recommendation, it's not just us trying to cover our butts."

Thirty days after the report was issued, US Rep. Candice Miller (R-MI) proposed legislation that would authorize the Corps to close the hydrological connection between the Mississippi River and the Great Lakes. The legislation died in committee.

According to Tim Eder, the executive director of the Great Lakes Commission in Ann Arbor, there are two concerns with the permanent barrier: time and money. Twenty-five years is way too long to wait for a permanent solution, and the dollar amount presented by the Corps is inflated because it includes the multibillion-dollar tab for Chicago to finally fix its wastewater problem.

The Great Lakes Commission's preferred long-term solution, Eder says, is to restore the natural divide by constructing barriers in four different locations on the Chicago Area Waterway System: the Chicago River, the Calumet River, the Grand Calumet River, and the Little Calumet River.

In 2012, the commission issued a report that said it was possible to restore the natural divide, stop the two-way flow of invasive species, provide flood protection, fix Chicago's wastewater problem, and maintain cargo traffic all at the same time.[11] The plan would require costly improvements to one of the city's four water-treatment plants. The construction of four barriers would require the construction of a transfer terminal, since barges would no longer be able to move from Lake Michigan into the Cal Sag Channel, which connects the CSSC with Lake Michigan through the Calumet River on the lake's southwest side. Building that terminal would not impact barge traffic all that much, Eder says, because most barges work within the river system and never enter Lake Michigan or travel all the way to the Mississippi River.

Overall, the project would cost between $3.2 billion and $9.5 billion, but only a small fraction of the cost is in the physical barrier; most of the cost goes into flood protection, transportation, and sewage-treatment improvements. Before any barrier can be constructed, however, Chicago will need to deal with its wastewater problem. Current levels of treatment do not meet the EPA's regulations for wastewater discharge.

Robert Reichel of the Michigan attorney general's office believes the Great Lakes Commission has developed a sound proposal. He also believes that the US Army Corps of Engineers has systematically exaggerated the extent of the commerce and economic impact of transportation through the CAWS, which ends up positing a false choice—the cost of protection of the Great Lakes versus a loss of commerce that has had its value inflated.

Eder says that although the Great Lakes Commission has not fully rejected separation as the preferable option, the Great Lakes Commission is working with the Great Lakes states to reach an agreement. The commission is holding regular meetings with representatives from state governments and has even brought in a facilitator to help find common ground and maybe even reach a settlement. "We said we believe that physical separation is best but want the federal government to determine how it will work," Eder says.

"How do we accommodate transportation, rainwater, and sewage? How do we do this without flooding downtown Chicago?"

———

So if a political solution is a ways off and the electric barrier has faults that may or may not be corrected, what is to keep the carps from reaching the Great Lakes? Maybe the states should just sue the US Army Corps of Engineers and get a judge to order the canal closed.

That strategy was tried—and rejected. In 2012, Michigan, Wisconsin, Minnesota, Ohio, Pennsylvania, and the Grand Traverse Band of Ottawa and Chippewa Indians sued the US Army Corps of Engineers to force the federal government to build barriers on the CAWS that would permanently separate the Great Lakes from the Mississippi basin. But in December 2012, US District Judge John Tharp threw out the states' lawsuit because federal law requires the Corps to keep shipping channels open between the lakes and the river. In his written ruling, Tharp said the court was "mindful of, and alarmed by, the potentially devastating ecological, environmental, and economic consequences that may result from the establishment of an Asian carp population in the Great Lakes," but the proper channel for remediation was not through the courts but through Congress.[12]

The states' appeal of Tharp's decision received only a puzzling rejection. In deciding not to hear the appeal, Diane Wood, the chief judge for the U.S. Court of Appeals for the Seventh Circuit, wrote, "We do not want to be understood as taking this problem lightly. We have proceeded throughout on the assumption that the introduction of Asian carp to Lake Michigan would pose a grave threat to the public's use and enjoyment of the Great Lakes." But, Wood said, there is "a notable lack of factual allegations that Asian carp are passing or are about to pass the barriers that the Corps has established, and the complaint does not plausibly allege that the Corps cannot or will not respond to more urgent threats if and when they arise. To the contrary, the allegations tend to show that the Corps is taking its stewardship over the CAWS and the carp problem seriously."[13] In other words, the judge said to come back when it's too late.

Robert Reichel of the Michigan attorney general's office understands why judges are reluctant to resolve complex interstate disputes where there is already federal involvement and perceived expertise on the part of the federal government. Nevertheless, he says that despite the legal setback, the Michigan attorney general's office will continue to prod the federal government to move toward the best solution: hydrological separation. "Ultimately it's going to take congressional action to close the Chicago Area Waterway

System," Reichel says. "Litigation is not an ideal tool for solving complex environmental problems."

One solution for lowering the risk to the Great Lakes is to fish down the carp population in the Illinois River. With fewer carps in the river, it's less likely one or more will make it across the electric barriers in the Chicago Sanitary and Ship Canal. So to reduce carp numbers, the state of Illinois has hired commercial fishermen who usually work in other parts of the state to remove huge numbers of carp from five different sections of the Illinois River. One of those areas is centered on William G. Stratton State Park on the banks of the Illinois River in Morris, Illinois.

It's the first day of December, it's overcast, and the air temperature is well below freezing and will be all day. But there is still fishing to do, and Gary Shaw is ready to go. It's before eight a.m., and already five fishing boats have been launched from their trailers underneath the State Road 47 bridge over the river and are now lined up on the shore. Today they are fishing a backwater along the Illinois River that was created by a nearby sand-mining operation.

Despite a slight breeze, the water is calm. Wearing forest-green waterproof clothing and a camouflage hat with ear flaps, Shaw climbs into his thirty-foot aluminum fishing boat that provides no shelter from the cold or wind and no place to sit. The flat-bottom boat is divided into three compartments—one for nets, buoys, and anchors; one for the fish; and one for the pilot. The nicest thing about this boat is the massive two-hundred-horsepower Suzuki four-stroke engine that will become an important weapon in the coming battle with the carp.

Shaw is shortly joined by his deckhand, Ed Schoenhard, and Blake Bushman, a natural-resource coordinator with the Illinois Department of Natural Resources. Once everybody is on board, Shaw backs the boat away from shore, hits the gas, and heads downstream. His is among the first boats out.

After just a few minutes, and still within view of the State Road 47 bridge, Shaw turns left and heads out of the river's main channel and into the backwater. It's evident that this is an industrial area—there are rusting barges along the shore, and the shoreline is littered with plastic jugs and containers and other trash. Despite the lack of aesthetics, this water body draws carps in by the hundreds because it's out of the river's current and is a place where fish can tuck in and expend less energy during a time of the year when there is little for them to eat.

Shaw noses the boat up to the shore, and Schoenhard throws out an anchor attached to one end of a gill net. Shaw puts the motor into reverse and directs the boat on a path that will lay the net in a shape that resembles a comma. Rather than setting a net in a straight line, the strategy is to lay the

Blake Bushman estimates the weight of a bighead carp that had been caught in the Illinois River minutes earlier. It's a big fish, but in the right conditions, a bighead carp can grow much bigger.

net in a spiral, zigzag, or some other shape or pattern. It's easier to catch the fish if they are driven into an enclosed area.

Once the three-hundred-yard net is laid out, the herding begins. Of course, it begs the question, how does someone herd something that can't be seen in the murky water below? The question is answered when Bushman and Schoenhard pick up small aluminum bats and bang on the boat, and Shaw raises the motor so that the propeller is just inches under water. Once the propeller is in position, Shaw revs the motor up and down rapidly. The sounds and vibrations will scare the fish and force them to swim into the nets as they try to escape.

Despite all the clanging and revving, there are no jumping carps today; the water is too cold for the fish to be active.

After about five minutes of clanging and revving, it's time to bring in the net. There are fish, all right—buffaloes, drums, and channel catfish, which are extracted carefully and thrown back in the water. The first three carps to come in aren't bighead or silver—they're common carps. Finally, Schoenhard hauls in the first bighead carp, weighing about ten pounds, followed shortly by a silver carp. The fish are extracted from the nets with not nearly so much care and are tossed into a compartment in the middle of the boat. Soon, the entire length of the net is on board, and there's disappointment all around; the set produces only one bighead and thirteen silver carps.

Now that the fish are in, it's time for Bushman to go to work. The biologist is on board for three reasons. First, he'll gather data that will help the Illinois DNR make decisions about future efforts: what net lengths and heights are best, how many fish are caught in a certain location, how many fish are caught based on the amount of effort. Second, there is no commercial fishing on this stretch of the Illinois River, and Bushman is there to ensure all the native fish are returned. Third, the biologist is there to ensure that none of the carps are misappropriated. In 2014, the Illinois DNR arrested the owner of a Grafton, Illinois, fish market after he sold live bighead carps to an undercover agent. In an effort to curtail the spread of Asian carps, the state of Illinois has made it a felony to possess or sell a live Asian carp. If found guilty, the market's owner faced five years in prison and a $25,000 fine.

While Bushman is counting, Shaw looks for another place to set a net. Even though Shaw has been fishing all his life and he's an old hand at this type of fishing, he views it as a game of wits. He says he has seen bighead and silver carps swim right up to the nets, eye them with suspicion, and swim away. Then there have been those hot summer days when he can see the water roiling with struggling carps because so many have been caught in one set. That, he says, is pretty satisfying.

Besides being a game of wits, fishing for carps has become personal. Bighead and silver carps have displaced the native fish in Shaw's downstate rivers and have cut into his profits. In addition, the carps, because of their weight and size, damage his nets, which increases his costs.

There's a saying that a bad day of fishing is better than a good day at the office, but after three additional sets, Shaw may be considering a desk job. With the lack of fish, the men start recounting stories of previous carp-hunting excursions. There was the time when they brought in eight hundred pounds of fish. There was the story about when all the boats were so loaded down with carps that the water was lapping at the gunwales. There were the stories about the friendly wagers over who would catch the biggest or the most carps. As you would expect, the language is salty, and the stories are often embarrassing.

Today, however, a quick look around shows all the boats in the area are riding high, which means everybody is pretty much struggling. It could be that this area is fished out, or it could be that it's so cold that the fish are just not very active. Or it could be that the fish have schooled up and left the area. Or because the water is clearer, perhaps the fish can see the nets and avoid them. No matter the reason, everyone who is part of this effort will tell you it's just tougher to fish this time of year. Despite the cold, there is one advantage to fishing this time of year—the multiple layers of clothing prevent the fishermen from getting covered with smelly fish slime during the course of the day.

The morning is getting late, but there's time for one more set before they'll call it a day. Shaw once again noses his boat up to the shore, and Schoenhard throws the anchor into the sand and starts to feed out the net. Shaw then backs up the boat and makes a large loop, laying out twelve hundred yards of net, and the clanging and revving begins once again. After five minutes, it's time to retrieve the net. Like the other sets, the early returns are discouraging; there's nothing in the first couple hundred yards of net. But as the net winds around into the deeper part of the lake away from shore, Shaw starts to haul in fish. At first, they come in ones and twos, every ten feet or so. Soon, the fish start coming in groups of threes and fours every few feet. Before too much longer, Shaw begins to struggle with the net, and he pulls in a group of four fish, including one bighead carp that's nearly three feet long and weighing upward of thirty-five pounds. This is much closer to what they would expect to catch on a normal day.

The haul nets 5 bighead and 112 silver carps, which more than triples what had been previously caught earlier in the day, and it takes some of the sting out of what had been a pretty unproductive morning.

(Even though it was a relatively unproductive morning along this stretch of the Illinois River, on the same day, twenty-five miles downstream near Ottawa, Illinois, fishermen hit the jackpot, catching an estimated one hundred thousand pounds of carp in a seine net in a single haul. Wildlife managers estimated that at one time they had five hundred thousand pounds of carp in the net, but several thousand fish escaped when a portion of the net broke under the weight.)

It's only a five-minute high-speed run back to the boat ramp. The boats are put on trailers and lined up underneath the Illinois State Road 47 bridge, and the fish are off-loaded into bins and lifted into a refrigerated semitrailer that is parked nearby. Soon, they will be shipped off to a processing plant to be made into liquid fertilizer. Bushman, meanwhile, starts working with three other Illinois DNR biologists to measure and weigh a representative sample for more data.

From this stretch of the river alone, in 2014, the Illinois DNR estimates that the fishing operation has removed more than 11,300 bighead and 54,411 silver carps. The fishermen, however, are paid by the pound. Instead of counting individuals, they see it as having removed 314 tons of fish. Farther down the river, the fishing program has removed approximately 375 tons of Asian carps from the Marseilles and Starved Rock pools during the same calendar year.

The fishing project is one of twenty-one different projects to monitor Asian carps and reduce the possibility that they will cross into Lake Michigan. The state has established six monitoring projects above and below the fish barrier, along with four different barrier-effectiveness projects. The state is also looking for carps in urban ponds and fish-stocking projects. "We shut the front door, but we don't want them going to the back door," says Kevin Irons of the Illinois DNR.

Fishing will continue until the river freezes over. And despite the cold, Shaw will be out every day, because there's fishing to do.

The Illinois DNR is not alone in fishing for the carp. Every summer, a group of eager volunteers hits the Illinois River near the town of Bath, Illinois, for what has become a legendary event: the Original Redneck Fishing Tournament. The goal of the tournament is to catch as many jumping silver carps as possible using only handheld dip nets in two-hour free-for-all heats. Of course, given the number of boats on the river at any one time, the carps are particularly agitated, and participants are at risk of broken noses or other injuries when being blindsided by a twenty-pound fish.

The jumping carps have become such an attraction that there are now silver carp fishing charters for bow hunters on the Illinois River. Dan O'Keefe of Michigan Sea Grant is concerned, however, because he has heard rumblings about how overzealous bow hunters have transported silver carps into Lake Michigan in hopes that they could ultimately be hunted there. Any effort to establish the carp in Lake Michigan for hunting purposes would be futile, O'Keefe says. The carps jump as a fear response to the boats on a narrow river, but in much larger and deeper Lake Michigan, the carps would simply swim away.

———

Fishing down the bighead and silver populations and converting the fish into fertilizer or food for other fish or even for human consumption seems like an example of making lemonade when life hands you lemons. Since there are excessive numbers of these fish in the river, doesn't it make sense to find a creative way to use the resource?

There are multiple reasons why people are in favor of fishing Asian carps from North American waterways: they're ugly; they're dangerous when they jump; they're a nuisance to boaters; there are too many of them; they displace native fish; there's a risk they could spread into the Great Lakes. Now, there's another reason: they are profitable.

Companies from Illinois to Mississippi are already processing and selling the wild-caught carps to markets as far away as China, and others are lining up to do the same. In late 2014, the city council in Pekin, Illinois, discussed whether the city should fund a study on whether there was a local market for Asian carps as food after receiving several inquiries from companies considering whether to develop fish-processing plants in the town of thirty-four thousand people.

But Becky Cudmore wonders, if you create a market—an entire economy—around something that you prefer to eliminate or eradicate, do you risk perpetuating their existence? The consensus of opinion right now is that nobody wants the carps in North American watersheds, and there's no Asian carps lobby to defend the fish, but will that change when jobs and workers' livelihoods depend on them?

Multiple companies are already fishing for, processing, and selling the carps or are making plans to. In 2014, a Kentucky company announced it would create 110 new jobs and invest $18.7 million in an Asian carps project.

The idea of making a resource out of something that many people would like to see eliminated from the North American watershed is something that Kevin Irons of the Illinois DNR has considered and discussed with other state policy makers. The conclusion, Irons says, was that fishing down the carps and treating them as a resource had both ecological and economic benefits that outweighed the ethical concerns. "We want to fish them to extinction, but we're not likely to fish these guys out," Irons says. Given how the carps have become established in rivers large and small from Minnesota to Louisiana, and from South Dakota to Pennsylvania, it's not likely we are ever going to have the opportunity to eliminate them.

Chipping in to control bighead and silver carps and make a buck at the same time is Philippe Parola, a chef and restaurant consultant in Baton Rouge, Louisiana. Parola has found a way to debone and prepare the carps to make them tasty and affordable enough to meet Americans' demands. Besides developing a marketing plan for the carps, Parola serves nutria, which is also known as coypu, a South American rodent that is now widely hated throughout bayous in the southern United States for its destructive feeding and burrowing habits. Parola admits that even though the fish is high in protein and low in fat and has less mercury than tuna, he still needed to make the carps more palatable to North American tastes. With that in mind, Parola now markets the carp as "silverfin."

Parola is not alone in his attempts to improve the image of the fish. In other parts of the United States, grass carp is being marketed as white amur, and bighead carp is being called "noble fish" in a play on its scientific name, *Hypophthalmichthys nobilis*. In other areas along the Mississippi River, the bighead and silver carps are being marketed as "Kentucky whitefish." To get people to overcome the fear of bones in their fish, an Illinois company has developed a system that presses a carp filet against a wire mesh. The skin and bones mostly stay on one side of the mesh, and the flesh comes through on the other side with the texture of raw ground turkey. Although the meat does taste a little fishy, blind taste tests in Missouri have shown that people prefer the carps over the state's most popular aquatic meal, catfish.

North America's Asian American community doesn't need to be convinced. In Chinese neighborhoods in Chicago, Toronto, and New York City, the carps are considered a delicacy. Buyers want the fish alive and still swimming and are willing to pay top dollar for a live carp. In fact, in early 2015 the Illinois DNR was allowing shippers to bring as much as five thousand pounds of live sterile grass carp into Chicago on a weekly basis. The DNR viewed this inflow of sterile grass carp as a calculated risk. By allowing the sterile carp into Chicago's Asian markets, the agency hoped to prevent people from driving to Missouri, where fertile grass carp are sold across the counter. But now that the bighead and silver carps are listed as an injurious species under the Lacey Act of 1900, interstate transport of live fish is mostly illegal. Carole Engle, the director of aquaculture at the University of Arkansas at Pine Bluff, told the *Detroit Free Press* in 2011 that the ban on those carp shipments put a $100 million dent in the US economy, hurting fish farmers, haulers, and markets.[14]

Ontario has now outlawed the possession of live Asian carps, but as recently as 1996, Ontario imported nearly two hundred thousand pounds of grass carp and more than a million pounds of bighead carp into the greater Toronto area alone. Given the economics, there's strong incentive to smuggle live carps into Canada. So it wasn't surprising that in 2014, a driver and his Alberta-based trucking company were fined a total of $75,000 in Canadian currency after the driver twice tried to enter Canada through Windsor, Ontario, in 2012, hauling live grass and bighead carps and other fish from Arkansas. Although the fish were on ice, a close inspection by an Ontario conservation officer found that some of the fish were still alive. Ontario wildlife managers suspected that the driver left Arkansas with a trailer carrying live fish in water and replaced the water with ice shortly before reaching the Canadian border at the Ambassador Bridge. Once clear of the border, the driver was planning to refill the trailer with water to deliver the fish to Toronto still alive.

Because bighead and silver carps can survive for many hours without water and can look dead without being dead, they have earned the nickname "zombie fish."

———

Fishing down the population is having an impact on the number of carps in the Illinois River, and research on an additional fatal control technique is under way at the US Geological Survey's facility in Columbia, Missouri.

The USGS is experimenting with food spiked with Antimycin, an incredibly deadly piscicide. Robin Calfee, of the USGS, says the delivery of poison through food has been used in the aquaculture industry for many years.

Of course, there are multiple challenges with developing a piscicide for this application. First, the carps are in the wild and not in an enclosed facility, so the biggest challenge is developing a particle that's large enough to hold the toxin yet small enough to be a size the carps prefer without poisoning other fish. Silver and bighead carps are both filter feeders that generally consume particles between sixty and one hundred microns in size. That's a good size because native paddlefish like to eat particles a little larger, and buffaloes like particles that are smaller. Unfortunately, gizzard shad, another native fish in the river, like to eat particles in the same size range as the carps.

So to prevent a mass accidental poisoning of the gizzard shad population, the researchers are experimenting with a particle that will release the toxin only if it comes in contact with protease, an enzyme that is present in a silver carp's gut but is either not present or present in tiny amounts in a gizzard shad's digestive system. It appears this could be a very effective way of delivering toxins to large numbers of bighead and silver carps as the USGS has discovered that the wild carps will quickly become habituated and gather in large numbers if they are fed by humans at regular times. Getting fish habituated to a regular feeding time could be helpful because concentrating fish in a small area could also help commercial fishermen improve their catch rate.

There's one other problem: what happens if that toxic particle falls apart before it's ingested by the carps? If more than 3 percent of the Antimycin leaches from the particles, there could be a problem. In controlled tests, it took only one one-thousandth of a part per billion of Antimycin to kill half the paddlefish in an enclosed space.

Despite the promise, Calfee stresses that the toxic particles are not a silver bullet. "We're not going to go out into the Mississippi and spread it all over," Calfee says. "It's one of the tools within an integrated system" that includes using flashing lights, sounds, and bubbles to influence fish movement. Calfee and other scientists with the USGS are experimenting with those techniques in both Columbia and La Crosse, Wisconsin, and they may soon be part of a new effort to prevent carp movement at the Brandon Road Lock and Dam on the Des Plaines River just south of Joliet, Illinois. The Brandon Road Lock and Dam is a natural choke point for the carps, as most of the river is blocked by a twenty-five-foot-high dam. The only way for a carp to get above the dam is through the locks that transport the barges between the two elevations. To keep the carps from being transported above the dam, researchers may soon be placing an array of bubble curtains, lights, and acoustic devices near the lower gates to discourage the fish from entering.

Dan Zielinski, a postdoctoral associate at the University of Minnesota's Aquatic Invasive Species Research Center, has been working on developing carp deterrence strategies in the locks on the Mississippi River near Genoa, Wisconsin. Zielinski believes acoustic deterrents have good potential because the carps can hear sounds at a wider frequency range and their hearing is more sensitive than most native fish species. In his research, Zielinski used common carps as surrogates and experimented with three different types of bubble curtains. Trials showed the bubble curtains reduced fish passage by as much as 85 percent. Zielinski believes the carps avoided the bubble curtain in response to the sound of the bubbles and the motion of the water rather than being deterred visually.

Of course, the installation of carp-deterrence devices at Brandon Road Lock comes with trade-offs. First, it will likely impede the movement of native species, and, second, it will only block the movement of invasive species from the Mississippi basin to the Great Lakes basin and do nothing to prevent the movement of invasives traveling in the opposite direction.

All of this control comes at a pretty steep price. In a 2014 report to Congress, FWS reported that between June 2012 and June 2014, the federal and state governments spent more than $94 million on carp-control efforts. The US Army Corps of Engineers alone spent more than $51 million, the US Geological Survey spent more than $11 million, and the state of Illinois spent more than $10 million.

There's one other form of control developing: natural predators. A 2014 study by researchers and students at Western Illinois University found young Asian carps in the stomachs of channel catfish, flathead catfish, largemouth bass, white bass, black crappie, white crappie, and gar species.[15] The study was conducted in a small section of the Illinois River following an unusually large hatch of carps earlier in the season; so young carps were plentiful at that particular time, and native fish were simply taking advantage of an abundant prey item.

There's also evidence that the blue catfish, one of the largest fish in the Illinois and Mississippi Rivers, are now eating adult silver carps. In a Mississippi River backwater near Alton, Illinois, researchers discovered a spot where blue catfish were finding lots of silver carps to eat. Blue catfish are able to eat adult silver carps because they have an unusually large mouth, which makes them able to swallow fish up to twenty inches long.

In Burlington, Ontario, Becky Cudmore is performing control experiments similar to the USGS's in an old boat slip in Hamilton Harbor. Cudmore and her team have installed an array of lights and speakers in the three-sided slip. To keep the fish from escaping, a net has been drawn across the slip's open end.

Instead of using Asian carps as test subjects, Cudmore uses common carps caught in Hamilton Harbor as surrogates. She admits that even if she could bring in carps from the United States, she wouldn't be able to bring herself to import the real thing. The United States is doing its best to prevent the carps from entering the Great Lakes, she says. How would it look if they escaped into the lakes through Canada?

Cudmore's reluctance to import bighead and silver carps is understandable, because when it comes to Asian carps, the Canadian government is not messing around. In May 2012, the government of Prime Minister Stephen Harper announced C$17.5 million in funding for a new program to prevent Asian carps from becoming established. The program is built on four pillars: prevention, outreach, risk assessment, and monitoring and early warning. Canada already has a long history with invasives and has absorbed the lesson learned with the zebra mussel and sea lamprey invasions. With Asian carps lurking in the United States, Cudmore's agency has an opportunity and an obligation to prevent an invasion.

With that influx of money, DFO has opened a new laboratory in Cudmore's facility in Burlington and has allowed the agency to begin a monitoring program on rivers it considers most likely to attract Asian carps. That monitoring program paid dividends in the summer of 2014 when a grass carp was discovered in the Grand River near Dunnville, Ontario.

The discovery of any one of the four Asian carp species in Canadian waters triggers a rapid response from the DFO's SWAT team. Following the established framework for rapid response, the DFO immediately informed the provincial government, nearby state governments, and the US federal government. Then the agency went to work to determine whether the fish was sterile. The best way to check whether a dead fish is sterile, Cudmore says, is to analyze the fluid inside the eye, which she can now do inside her own lab instead of sending the eyes to FWS's lab in La Crosse, Wisconsin, for analysis. That allows her to have an answer on a fish's status in hours instead of days.

Even before determining that the fish was indeed sterile, the agency ordered electrofishing crews to search the river for other grass carps and to conduct eDNA tests. Water taken from the area immediately after the discovery contained grass carp eDNA, but within a few days, the tests could no longer detect grass carp DNA. With no other captures, only then the agency felt it was safe to stand down.

---

Cudmore and her staff were relieved that the Grand River grass carp was sterile, which gave them confidence that there was not an established population in the waterway. It's unknown how this carp got into the river, but it could be that this single fish was an escapee from an agricultural pond in Ohio or Pennsylvania, where it is legal to stock sterile grass carps.

In stocking agricultural ponds, Ohio was just doing what many other states were doing: using a low-impact, natural method to control aquatic plant growth. Not only did Ohio allow the stocking of sterile grass carps, but the state somewhat encouraged it. In 2009, Ohio State University's extension program published a fact sheet on the benefits of grass carps, calling them "a useful tool" in managing nuisance aquatic plants in ponds and small lakes. Although Ohio requires that the carps shipped into the state are sterile, a tiny minority of carps that get shipped to Ohio and elsewhere are fertile.

In aquaculture, reproduction of Asian carps often needs to be induced because in controlled settings, there are no spawning cues like a rapid rise in the water level and flow following a heavy rain. So to produce the next generation of carps, fish farmers induce spawning with hormones, then collect the fertilized eggs in a raceway or hatching jar. Almost immediately after the eggs are fertilized, they are exposed to a shock of high pressure and then a warm-water bath to render them sterile.

Every unfertilized egg has a pair of female chromosomes. When the egg is fertilized, the chromosomes reconfigure with one pair of male and one pair of female. The second pair of female chromosomes is now extra, and because apparently even for fish three's a crowd, the mated pair pushes the extra pair of female chromosomes out of the egg. Any fish with male and female chromosomes is called a *diploid* and will grow up to be a normal, healthy fish that is able to breed. But any fish hatched from an egg with three pairs of chromosomes is a *triploid* and will grow up to be a normal, healthy fish that is sterile. The process of making eggs into triploid fish has a success rate of more than 99.5 percent, which means in a batch of a thousand fish, fewer than five will be diploid.

But it doesn't take many diploid fish to establish a breeding population. A 2011 risk assessment by DFO[16] showed there was more than a 50 percent chance that a breeding population could be established in any of the Great Lakes with just twenty fish—ten males and ten females.

That may have been exactly what happened in the Sandusky River. That river, which is an important tributary to Lake Erie in northern Ohio, now appears to be home to an established grass carp population, the first in the Great Lakes basin. In 2013, commercial fishermen caught four fertile grass carps in the river. Scientists know these carps had spent their entire lives in the river by analyzing the tiny bones in the fish's ears. The ear bones, which are called otoliths, grow in concentric circles like the rings of a tree, and their chemical structures reflect the water chemistry. Nobody knows how long the adults that spawned this generation of carps have been in the river or how many generations there are now, but biologists speculate it's possible their ancestors go back to the early 1980s, when it was legal to stock agricultural ponds in Ohio with fertile fish, according to Jeff Tyson, the Lake Erie fisheries program administrator for the Ohio DNR.

Even though the grass carps are largely confined to the river, which would make them easier to find and eradicate, Dan O'Keefe of Michigan Sea Grant cautions that it would be a bad idea to poison vast stretches of the river because it could kill other fish that could potentially prey on—and control—the young carps.

The chances of fertile grass carps escaping into the wild have been greatly diminished since the early 1980s; all but a few states have since outlawed the stocking of fertile grass carps, and FWS established the National Triploid Grass Carp Inspection and Certification Program in Warm Springs, Georgia. The inspection program was authorized by Congress in 1995 "to provide assurance . . . that shipments of grass carp alleged to be all triploid, do not, within the confidence limits of the inspection program, contain diploids."[17]

When a batch of triploid grass carps is scheduled for shipment, an FWS inspector will travel to the fish farm to observe the producer's testing process. Out of a batch with a maximum of 6,000 fish, 120 fish chosen at random are tested for ploidy. A small amount of blood is taken from each of the 120 fish and is analyzed by a machine called a Coulter Counter. The Coulter Counter doesn't actually test for chromosomes in cells; it tests for resistance caused by particle size. Triploids have larger blood cells because they contain one and a half times the DNA of diploids, so if the Coulter Counter detects more resistance, it determines the blood is from a triploid fish. If any one of the tested fish is determined to be a diploid, the entire lot fails inspection, and the producer must retest every fish in the batch before they can be shipped.

In a three-year period ending in 2014, FWS inspectors checked 592 lots of grass carp for ploidy. Two of the lots failed the inspection and were not released, but more than a million triploid grass carps were ultimately distributed to twenty-nine states.

On the surface, a grass carp ploidy inspection program sounds great. In reality, the program has one major flaw: it's voluntary. According to Bill Wayman, the director of the Warm Springs Fish Technology Center, which is home to the inspection program, only a small portion of the southern fish farms that produce grass carps participate in the inspection program.

So here's where we stand: The Great Lakes are at risk. Illinois is unlikely to close the CAWS anytime soon because of what it means to the state's economy. Courts are unwilling to intervene because they believe this issue is up to Congress. Carp-control techniques are limited and flawed, and millions of dollars have been spent to install a barrier that may or may not be effective. The Army Corps of Engineers does what Congress tells it to do, and Congress shows no sign of wanting to spend billions of dollars on permanent separation.

So if it's difficult to create invasive-species policy that satisfies all parties when it's just states and the federal government involved, try adding the interests of another country into the mix.

# 8

# POLICY

With almost military precision, the briefing started at 7:30 a.m. on a chilly, overcast September morning. With maps posted on tent walls and spread out on tables, Kevin Irons, the invasive-species coordinator from the Illinois Department of Natural Resources, and Eric Fischer, Indiana's coordinator, laid out the mission.

Boats would start entering the water of Calumet Harbor on the Indiana-Illinois border shortly after 7:30 a.m. Each boat would take a defined area based on its capability: electrofishers in the shallow nearshore waters; trawlers and net setters in the deeper water offshore.

Even though this was marketed as the first multistate invasive-species exercise following the adoption of a mutual aid agreement signed by Great Lakes governors and premiers in April 2014, it was an exercise with a purpose: Eurasian ruffe eDNA was found in this harbor the previous year. It's possible that the ruffe DNA was transported into the harbor in the ballast water of a lake freighter coming down from Duluth, Minnesota, but it's also possible that there's now an established population in Calumet Harbor. Either way, it was time to find out.

Despite a moderate northeasterly wind coming across Lake Michigan, the water had only a mild chop. One by one, the boats from the departments of natural resources from Indiana, Illinois, Wisconsin, and Michigan; the Illinois Natural History Survey; the US Geological Survey; and the US Fish and Wildlife Service (FWS) entered the water and motored to their assigned spots to being the search.

As the sun rose higher, a lighter shade of gray broke through a darker one, eventually allowing the smoke and steam from the steel mills of Gary and the refineries of Whiting, Indiana, to become one with the clouds.

A crew from the Indiana Department of Natural Resources does electroshock fishing in an exercise designed to search for invasive species in Calumet Harbor on the Indiana-Illinois border. The multistate, multiagency exercise is designed to be a rapid response to the discovery of any additional nonnative species that might be found in the Great Lakes or a tributary in the future.

Throughout the morning, fishing crews worked back and forth in the harbor, and local TV crews came and went. By early afternoon, as the crews began to finish their assignments and come ashore for a debriefing, confidence began to grow that there were no ruffe here.

Even though this exercise failed to find any Eurasian ruffe, it was deemed a success for what it found—a way for all these agencies from different states and jurisdictions to work together as one unit. This training exercise was the first activity following the announcement of a mutual agreement signed in April 2014 by the governors of the Great Lakes states and the premiers of Ontario and Quebec. That agreement allowed states and provinces to pool their resources to respond to the discovery of a new species in a specific location in the Great Lakes—essentially taking a SWAT-team approach. The training session also demonstrated how Great Lakes states and provinces, and not the federal governments, are leading the way on aquatic-invasive-species policy.

———

Invasive species have become a hot topic among Great Lakes politicians on both sides of the border. Governors and premiers vow to protect the lakes from the introduction of additional organisms and to control the ones that are already here, and legislators tell their concerned constituents that they're doing everything they can; but, in essence, their efforts to stop the spread of invasives control is almost akin to a game of underwater Whac-A-Mole.

It turns out that it is possible for government to react quickly to new threats to the Great Lakes, if the following conditions are met:

- Their elected leaders work to harmonize policies across borders.

- They institute policies that are preventive and not reactive.

- They give agency employees the authority to pool their resources across state and national borders to act quickly to the discovery of a new species.

If a new species is discovered going forward, state and provincial governments will now work together to respond quickly with a predetermined command structure and framework. Prior to this agreement, it would have been nearly impossible for Michigan, say, to send help into Ohio or for Indiana and Illinois to join together in an effort to smoke out some newly discovered organism.

At the time the agreement was signed, the governors and premiers also released a list of eleven animals and five plant species—a least-wanted list—and announced they would jointly work together to ensure these species do not enter the ecosystem. The development of a least-wanted list is a milestone because it reflects the leaders' move to agree on something very basic: which species will be restricted or prohibited across the basin. Up until then, there was no such consensus, and the result was a mishmash of species regulation. As of June 2012, prior to the release of the list of the sinister sixteen, only the Asian carps and the snakehead were banned in the eight Great Lakes states and Ontario. Other feared and highly destructive species were prohibited in some states but not in others. For example, the yabby, a type of crayfish that was included on the dishonor roll, was outlawed only in Illinois, Minnesota, and Ohio. The wels catfish, which was also on the least-wanted list, wasn't prohibited anywhere. Since the announcement of the least-wanted list, many of the states have banned the species on the list, and the others were expected to follow.

The mutual aid agreement that provided the catalyst for the Calumet Harbor training session was drafted by Peter Johnson, the deputy director of the Council of Great Lakes Governors, a Chicago-based nonpartisan organization. With help from Kevin Irons of the Illinois DNR and Tammy Newcomb, a senior water-policy adviser and fisheries research biologist with the Michigan DNR, Johnson hammered out the agreement in only eleven months. Getting an international agreement approved in such a short amount of time is almost unheard of, but it's a reflection of how critical the leaders view this issue.

The agreement was announced at a meeting of the Council of Great Lakes Governors on Mackinac Island in 2014. While the political leaders were all handshakes and backslaps in front of the cameras, plans for the Calumet Harbor exercise were already well under way, and the people inside state agencies were quietly thrilled at finally having the ability to overcome hurdles that limited their effectiveness.

Specifically, the agreement authorizes state employees to work across state lines and addresses nuts-and-bolts issues like workers' compensation, lines of authority, costs associated with travel and equipment, the creation of common forms for record keeping, and the development of communication channels among agencies. "The whole idea is we don't have to spend a lot of time working this out at the last minute when something bad happens," Johnson says.

———

On both sides of the US-Canada border, the goals for invasive species are identical: prevention, detection, response, and management. Still, both countries are slowed by the structure of government itself and issues surrounding federal versus local authority. The problem is worse on the US side, where the lack of coordination makes it more difficult for policy makers, biologists, agency employees, and contracted researchers to make decisions and enforce laws.

In the US, the states have primary responsibility for invasive-species control and prevention, but their ability to prevent the importation of certain species is hampered by the US Constitution. The federal government, meanwhile, expects the states to be responsible for their own territories in a chain of lakes they share with other states and another country.

Making things worse, invasive-species policy, on the federal level at least, revolves around a piece of legislation that is more than one hundred years old, the Lacey Act of 1900. Of course, when that legislation was written, no one had conceived of the idea of "invasive species." That legislation, however, was farsighted enough to envision that there were animals and plants out there that were not welcome in the United States. Specifically, the Lacey Act gave the US Department of Agriculture the ability to prohibit the import and introduction of wildlife that is considered injurious to humans, agriculture, and the indigenous wildlife of the United States, and it also supports state laws that protect birds and wild game. Even though states had their own legislation that prohibited the illegal taking of wildlife, those laws were only partially effective. Poachers were killing animals—particularly birds—by the thousands and secretly shipping them across state borders for disposal in food markets and the fashion industry because even though it was illegal to shoot birds in one state, it was *not* illegal to sell them in another. The Lacey Act extended the state laws into interstate commerce and made it a federal crime to ship illegally taken animals across borders.

This new *federal* ability to halt interstate shipments of illegally taken animals was critically important because the commerce clause of the US Constitution makes it clear that only the federal government can regulate trade among the states unless Congress explicitly delegates that authority to the states. Because of the commerce clause, states could not stop interstate shipments of the illegally killed animals, even if they wanted to. The Lacey Act gave the federal government the authority to step into that gap, and when the interstate sales of illegally killed animals ended, so did the slaughter.

The commerce clause was included in the US Constitution in reaction to the failures of the Articles of Confederation. That document, adopted in 1781, gave the states the ability to regulate commerce, and many of them took maximum advantage of it, adopting high tariffs and other exclusionist measures to protect certain industries from interstate competition. When a young nation realized the Articles of Confederation needed to be scrapped in favor of a more effective document, the framers of the Constitution made sure only the federal government had the power to regulate trade among the states, with the intent of ensuring competition and not protectionism.

Because only the federal government has the power to regulate interstate commerce, states have to walk a fine line between protecting their environments and not blocking commerce. Here's a hypothetical situation to demonstrate: State A has a strong aquatic-plant industry. Businesses related to that industry do a great job of supplying backyard ponds and aquariums within the state, and the elected officials in that state want to do everything they can to support that industry. But businesses in State B want to sell aquatic plants in State A but can't because State A says the imported plants *might* be contaminated with species that State A would find harmful. Under the commerce clause of the US Constitution, it would be unconstitutional for State A to restrict or prohibit trade in those plants, even with the suspicion that there might be injurious plants involved. But that does not mean states are defenseless when it comes to preventing the import of harmful species. The courts have upheld some state prohibitions on imports as not being overly protectionist; but they have done so on a case-by-case, I-know-it-when-I-see-it basis, and the burden is on the state to demonstrate there is a compelling reason to prevent the import.

That is exactly what happened in 2007, when a group of shipping companies challenged Michigan's laws requiring ballast water be treated prior to discharge. The federal court, however, dismissed the lawsuit, ruling that the state was only trying to protect its territorial waters and that the restrictions were not intended to be protectionist.

Although the Lacey Act helps states protect their wildlife and prevents the import of species that have been deemed injurious, its shortcomings are obvious. First, because the law does not specifically give authority for federal agencies to manage for invasive species, the Lacey Act cannot be used to prevent an organism's spread after it is established. Second, the rules behind the law are too slow and too reactive. There are only two ways to get a species named as injurious, and neither is easy. One takes an act of Congress. The second is by petitioning FWS. On average, it takes more than three years for the agency to make a decision.[1] Third, even though the Lacey Act prevents the importation of plants and animals that are considered *injurious*, it does so in an "innocent until proven guilty" way. That means it's okay to import thousands or millions of individuals in a species until that species has been proven to cause damage to native ecosystems. By that time, of course, it's usually too late. Finally, punishments for Lacey Act violations are notoriously light.

FWS in 1973 proposed a "clean list" approach, which would shift the burden to importers to prove that any new species brought into the country would not be injurious or risk becoming injurious. The proposal was so widely opposed that the agency quietly dropped it four years later, leaving the Lacey Act and all its flaws to be the guiding invasive-species legislation.

In February 2012, the last time the list of injurious wildlife was updated, it included only 236 species or families of closely related species, and only five more—all snakes—were under evaluation. Noticeably absent from the list was the quagga mussel, which legislators in the US West want to see added to the list as quickly as possible.

Several proposals have been floated to strengthen the Lacey Act, including giving FWS emergency power to put a species on the injurious-wildlife list without going through a lengthy review in advance.

Perhaps the strongest case made for amending the Lacey Act was a report titled "Broken Screens: The Regulation of Live Animal Imports in the United States," issued in 2007 by the Defenders of Wildlife, a Washington, DC–based nonprofit.[2] The report's principal author, Peter Jenkins, believes the Lacey Act still has huge gaps that allow noninvasive animals into the United States because they are not considered "injurious" even though they are potentially carrying diseases, parasites, and pesticides.

Jenkins wants any updates to the Lacey Act to be prevention focused, proactive, flexible, science based but practical, cooperative with the states, and self-supporting so that Congress knows how enactment will be funded. Jenkins says he has spoken to members of Congress about updating the Lacey Act and has received a sympathetic ear, but he is surprised the issue doesn't get more priority nationally. "It's funny. There are so many people working hard to keep illegal immigrants from crossing the border, but so few people are willing to stop organisms from coming in," Jenkins says.

———

The clean list approach is rapidly becoming the norm around the world in the fight against invasives. New Zealand and Australia have already adopted clean lists, and the United Kingdom has recently moved in that direction.

Ellen Marsden, a professor of fisheries at the University of Vermont, believes that it's time for North American jurisdictions to view all nonnatives as potentially invasive. "This is a place that we should be headed," Marsden says. "The idea that we can cheerfully bring in all kinds of species—that's not okay anymore. We should be more intelligent than that."

Marsden points to the round goby as the perfect example. Under the new risk-screening process set up by FWS, the round goby may have been imported into the United States legally instead of coming as a stowaway on a cargo ship. One of the measures of the risk screening is whether there is prior evidence of invasion in other parts of the world. The goby might not have raised red flags because prior to its establishment in the Great Lakes, there was no previous evidence that it had become invasive anywhere else. "Don't wait around to see if it will be bad!" Marsden says. "That's playing with fire."

The clean list approach is the direction the states seem to be heading, too. In 2004, the Environmental Law Institute, a nonprofit, nonadvocacy environmental group based in Washington, DC, issued a report laying out a roadmap for states to adopt a clean list approach. In the lame-duck session of 2014, the Michigan legislature voted to develop a list of permitted species. Every state has a list of prohibited species, but it appears this is the first time a state has developed a permitted species list. Two state agencies, the Department of Agriculture and Rural Development (MDARD) and the Department of Natural Resources, will do a review of all species in trade in the state over the previous five years and then create a risk-assessment program to screen and potentially block any additional species coming in through trade. The process doesn't necessarily mean that all the plants and animals that have been sold commercially in the past will get a free pass. While developing the list of permitted species, the DNR and MDARD have the power to perform a risk analysis on any species already in trade that raises a red flag. If the species fails to pass the risk assessment, it could end up being restricted.

This approach helps to shield the state from potential constitutional issues or accusations of protectionism. By exposing a plant or animal to a risk assessment, the state can demonstrate that it has a compelling reason to restrict trade.

———

So it's clear that the states are more agile when it comes to responding to the threat posed by aquatic invasive species, but there is one thing the US government does well: distribute money. With the establishment of the Great Lakes Restoration Initiative (GLRI) in 2010, Congress has allocated almost $2 billion between fiscal years 2010 and 2015 to clean up toxins in harbors and industrial sites, combat invasive species, improve the health of lakes by protecting watersheds from runoff, and restore wetlands. The goals of the GLRI are to make fish safe to eat, to ensure water is safe for drinking and recreation, to clean toxins from polluted areas, to eliminate harmful algal blooms, to prevent additional invasives from becoming established, to control existing invasive-species populations and prevent additional invasives from becoming established, and to restore native habitats.

Specifically, invasive-species money has been spread to federal agencies including the US Environmental Protection Agency, US Geological Survey, US Fish and Wildlife Service, and National Park Service. With the money the EPA was budgeted, it has been providing grants to universities, Indian tribes, and regional nonprofits to conduct research, set up sea lamprey barriers in rivers, and restore critical habitat. Among the achievements so far has been development of the Great Lakes Aquatic Nonindigenous Species Information System database, risk assessments for invasive carps, and the development of a model that forecasts the biological and economic impacts of future introductions of exotic organisms.

We're not talking pennies here, either. Money from GLRI funding spent on the control of Asian carps in the Ohio and upper Mississippi Rivers was more than $36 million between June 2012 and June 2014.

———

When it comes to taking issues to Congress, it's important that the region speaks with one voice, says Tim Eder of the Great Lakes Commission. Eder says he and other staff members of the commission spend a lot of their time working with policy makers to find common ground. Even though everybody wants to protect the Great Lakes, reaching a consensus on pressing issues—whether to close the Chicago Area Waterway System to prevent the spread of Asian carps, for example—isn't easy when there's so much at stake economically. "It takes a lot of listening and drafting and back-and-forth," Eder says. "But states realize they are stronger when they speak together. They come to the table with a spirit of working together that helps a great deal."

Allegra Cangelosi, the former president of the Northeast-Midwest Institute in Washington, DC, says members of Congress are now taking the issue of invasive species seriously—not just in the Great Lakes but also in the Chesapeake Bay and saltwater harbors on the Atlantic and Pacific coasts. When talking with members of Congress, Cangelosi says she doesn't need to persuade them that this is an important issue—they get it. "That's the beautiful thing about working on issues about the Great Lakes," Cangelosi says. "People get that it's an environmental and economic issue. It's a different dynamic in the Great Lakes."

Many members of Congress still don't have a deep understanding of the issues. They've heard fears about jumping carps from constituents, but generally speaking, they don't have time to delve into the issues surrounding tiny critters from some far-off place when they are dealing with issues of national security and the budget. To advance understanding, some scientists are entering the political arena or are framing their research in a way that will maximize benefits for the Great Lakes.

Andrew Mahon, a molecular ecologist at Central Michigan University, is among those scientists getting involved in the process. He has spent time learning how to conduct himself with the media and how to talk with politicians and aides to get his point across. He even traveled to the US Capitol to talk with members of Congress and their aides in the summer of 2013 in an attempt to round up support for Great Lakes issues. "In order to have the impact that is important—I know this sounds like a cheesy response—to make the world a better place and to have an impact on the Great Lakes, you need to be doing this stuff," Mahon says.

In the process, Mahon has discovered that there are ways to talk about science, and there are ways to talk about what the politicians and their staffers want to hear. Some congresspeople want to understand the science, while others don't. If those politicians aren't interested in the science, he changes the message to focus on the impact of invasive species—what they are going to cost taxpayers and the government in the long run.

Mahon grew up in St. Louis, Missouri, with no connection to the Great Lakes as a child. Now he looks at them with passion. "I want to do research that makes a difference," Mahon says. "If that means me dabbling in policy, great. The worst-case scenario is that we've at least got people talking about it."

Invasive species haven't just changed the Great Lakes; they've also changed the way science is conducted, says Reuben Keller at Loyola University Chicago. Previously, scientists often would conduct research on some obscure organism out of personal curiosity. Today, scientists are focusing more on questions that are being asked by the public and policy makers as a way of contributing knowledge and potential solutions to the issue.

Aquatic invasive species have been a hot research issue since the zebra mussel turned up, and money is usually available because a certain government agency wants to learn more about the impact of a specific organism. State funding for research grants was almost nonexistent after the economic downturn that began in 2008, but money began to flow again in 2010 with the GLRI. Keller views that funding as both an opportunity and an obligation. "As scientists, we rely on public money to do our research," Keller says. "Shouldn't we be applying our science to the most important questions of the day?"

Because the impacts of invasive species are both deep and wide, David Lodge of the University of Notre Dame has created a team of interdisciplinary researchers that includes an economist to answer the questions that government decision makers are asking.

Lodge realized many years ago, when he was chair of the National Invasive Species Advisory Committee, that there was a critical aspect missing from invasive-species research: people would ask him about the economic impact of a particular species, and he couldn't tell them the answers. Since maximizing goals with limited resources is priority one in the fight against invasive species, wildlife managers had trouble making good decisions. What was missing, Lodge concluded, were economists who could add a dollars-and-cents aspect to the impacts of invasives and control efforts. He's much more comfortable now that he and his colleagues are addressing the most important research questions and framing them in ways that will maximize impact and results.

———

Even though members of Congress have demonstrated concern, they haven't necessarily been on top of the issue, doing everything they can. Starting in the late 1980s, Congress has made several attempts to deal with invasive species, but its efforts have yielded mixed results. The Nonindigenous Aquatic Nuisance Prevention and Control Act (NANPCA) of 1990 was a good start, creating a national invasive-species task force and the Great Lakes Panel on Aquatic Nuisance Species and giving FWS, the Coast

Guard, and the National Oceanic and Atmospheric Administration important new responsibilities. The National Invasive Species Act, passed by Congress in 1996, replaced and amended NANPCA. Among other provisions, NISA gave the Coast Guard authority to manage ballast water to prevent the introduction and spread of nonindigenous species. Several attempts were made to reauthorize the NISA after it expired in 2002, including the comprehensive National Invasive Species Act of 2007. That legislation failed to be passed into law partially because it was opposed by several environmental groups that objected to a provision that prevented states from enacting laws that were more stringent than federal rules.

If the NISA of 2007 had passed, it would have been clear that the federal government would have supremacy when it comes to the regulation and control of invasive species. But it didn't, and that vacuum raises several questions: Where does the authority of the federal government end and the authority of the states begin? How much leeway do states have to act on their own when the federal government is unwilling to act? What is the role of the federal government? What role should the states play? The same questions are in play on the Canadian side of the border.

Currently, the national model in both countries is that the states and provinces are responsible for protecting their own ecosystems, and the federal government provides support through funding and some law enforcement under import laws. The model in the Great Lakes, however, is slightly different. The states and provinces are still primarily responsible, but the federal governments play a larger role because of the international border and ballast-water issues.

So if the relationships between states, the provinces, and the federal governments are complicated and complex, add on regulation from the International Maritime Organization and international treaties, and brains begin to explode.

Dale Bergeron, a maritime extension educator with Minnesota Sea Grant in Duluth, says there are two parts to the problem. The first is the gross complexity of the regulations. The second is regulations that are ineffective or unenforceable or have unintended consequences. Bergeron uses Michigan's ballast-water law as an example. The law was great in concept, he says, but it ended up being unenforceable because in reality the state has no way to punish an offender. If a ship discharges ballast water in state waters, the state would have to capture a sample from that discharge and test it to see if was untreated. By the time regulators received the results of the lab tests, the ship would likely have left port and be well outside the state's jurisdiction. It would be possible for the state to issue a civil violation akin to a traffic ticket to a ship or a shipping company, but there's no guarantee it will ever collect;

and the state has no authority to prevent a ship from leaving port or to board a ship for impoundment inside or outside its territorial waters.

———

Perhaps the weakest link in invasive-species prevention is law enforcement. Law-enforcement officers are not trained to recognize invasive species, and states, provinces, and the federal governments have not made enforcement major priorities through training and additional funding.

But occasionally, law enforcement does get involved in a high-profile way. In May 2012, the Michigan DNR got a tip that grass carp was being sold out of the back of a truck traveling across the Lower Peninsula. (It was fairly easy to identify since the truck had "GRASS CARP" painted in big red letters on the side.) When conservation officers received the tip, the truck had just left Holland, Michigan, on its way to Midland. In Midland, a conservation officer made an undercover purchase of two grass carps, which is when other officers moved in to make the arrest. In making the bust, officers discovered that the truck was carrying 112 grass carps. The driver eventually pleaded guilty to twelve felonies and received a sentence of five months in jail and paid a $2,000 fine. Even though conservation officers were able to confiscate more than a hundred grass carps in this case, they don't know how many prohibited species come into the state undetected.

Stephanie Showalter Otts of the National Sea Grant Law Center said her organization is working with the states to develop a collaborative project with law enforcement, assistant attorneys general, and invasive-species coordinators. Part of the project is to raise awareness among state attorneys general of the invasive-species issue and to persuade them to assign a member of their staff to be responsible for the issue. Engaging law enforcement and prosecutors early in the legislative and policy-making process rarely happens. "Some policy decisions have even been made without consulting [attorneys general]," Otts says. "If they are engaged early, they can identify red flags and help to get everybody on the same page."

Still, getting law enforcement's attention on this matter is difficult when there is no additional funding for this purpose, and officers usually have more important things to worry about than whether there might be a stray carp larva in the latest delivery to the local bait dealer.

———

If invasive-species policy in the United States is bad because of gaps and its patchwork nature, it's worse on the north side of the border. Until 2015, Canada was fighting invasive species with a patchwork of twenty provincial and federal laws, none of which were passed specifically to deal with invasive species or biosecurity. Both the Ontario and Canadian governments are playing catch-up. The Canadian federal government spends more than C$4 million annually on aquatic-invasive-species control efforts nationwide, and the signs of commitment are there; but the policy still lags.

Canada developed its first national aquatic-invasive-species strategy in 2004 but did not propose national regulations until December 2014. Those regulations, which took effect in June 2015, prohibit the import, possession, transportation, and release of several aquatic invasive species, including Asian carps, and prohibit the introduction of any aquatic species into any body of water where it's not indigenous unless it had been authorized. Even though the legislation takes a "black list" approach, it's important because it finally gave the Canadian Border Services Agency the ability to seize shipments. Before this legislation, if a shipment of live Asian carps crossed into Ontario destined for Toronto, border agents had to call Ontario conservation officers to take control of the fish.

In February 2014, Ontario's parliament proposed Canada's first comprehensive invasive-species legislation at any level. That legislation would give the provincial government the authority to ban the possession and transportation of certain species, gives the province's Ministry of Natural Resources a rapid-response framework, authorizes partnerships with other jurisdictions, and updates inspection and enforcement regulations.

Cross-border harmonization is under way, too. Agency employees, particularly those with Fisheries and Oceans Canada, are in talks with counterparts in the United States to improve coordination. In 1972, the United States and Canada negotiated the Great Lakes Water Quality Agreement, a pact that bound the two nations to restore and maintain the Great Lakes. Of course, that was prior to the arrival of invasive species through ballast water.

When the agreement was amended in 2012, the governments added language that committed them to developing a joint aquatic-invasive-species strategy to prevent the introduction of additional aquatic invasive species and to control or eradicate existing ones, to implement early detection and rapid-response initiatives, to implement a ballast-water discharge plan, to develop a way to assess the effectiveness of prevention programs, and to develop technologies and methods to increase effectiveness of control techniques.

The pace of cross-border collaboration is likely to increase in the coming years, according to Jon Allan, the director of Michigan's Office of the Great Lakes. He believes all levels of government are aware that good, strong partnerships are necessary because when it comes to protecting the lakes, no one entity can do it all.

Unfortunately, it does not appear that there will be regionally consistent laws in one area: boat inspections. Even though Minnesota and Wisconsin have instituted mandatory watercraft and trailer inspection programs, Michigan is not likely to have one anytime soon, as the state's attorney general has ruled that a similar program would violate the state's constitution.

———

Even the most ardent advocate of the Great Lakes has to admit that progress has been made. It's easy to argue that government moves too slowly, and in retrospect, more could have been done to prevent the arrival of some of the worst invasives. This shouldn't be surprising, however, because it's difficult to get elected officials to legislate to prevent a hypothetical problem.

But governments on both sides of the US–Canada border have reacted and taken steps to reduce the risk into the future. Is it enough? It is impossible to know. But in the here and now, there are more pressing questions, starting with these: How do you measure the health of the Great Lakes going forward? If invasive-species control is a goal, how much control is enough?

# CONCLUSION

It has been a long, hard slog for biologists, conservationists, anglers, and policy makers, but progress has been made in the war to protect the Great Lakes from invasive species.

Governments in the United States and Canada have approved legislation and developed new rules and programs to close off pathways by regulating ballast water, while biologists and government employees have been in the field, working with teachers and biological supply houses, pet stores and garden centers, sellers on the Internet, and the aquaculture industry to educate them and reduce risk.

So what have we learned over the past four decades?

First, we've learned that we can't go back. The nonnative species that are here now will be here for a very long time to come, if not forever.

We've come to realize that money spent on prevention is money well spent.

We now know that one of the best ways to fight invasive species is through region-wide cooperation and harmonization of laws and policies, and law enforcement must view invasive species as a higher priority.

We've learned that the Great Lakes ecosystem has ways of repairing itself after a new species enters, but being able to differentiate between which problems will eventually mitigate themselves and which problems need to be attacked with effort and ingenuity will be helpful in deciding where to spend limited dollars and focus resources.

We've learned that when studying the biology of all the creatures in the Great Lakes—native and introduced—we must always keep in mind that even the tiniest plankton species has an impact on everything else.

We've learned that there is more work to be done, and there's a role for individual citizens of the Great Lakes region. We must dispose of our bait properly; take the time to clean, drain, and dry our boats when pulling them from the water; and always be aware that human activity is the primary vector for the spread of invasives. We must also take a larger role in reminding our lawmakers that the Great Lakes must be protected; there's very little cost in writing a letter or calling a legislator, but think of the payoff!

Finally, we've learned that we *must always* be vigilant to protect our native species and prevent new introductions. Among the species still lurking out there are monkey goby, killer shrimp, and water lettuce. The monkey goby sounds like it might be a fish that sits on your shoulder and does cute tricks for a piece of banana, but it's not. The monkey goby is feared because, in its native range in the Black Sea, it carries parasites that can also infest humans. If it comes into the Great Lakes through ballast water, it's likely bringing its parasites with it. The killer shrimp might sound like it could be the Friday-night appetizer special at the neighborhood seafood joint, but this crustacean has been expanding its range throughout Europe, leaving a trail of dead zooplanktons in its wake. If it reaches the Great Lakes, not only will it eat zooplankton, but biologists fear it will also eat fish eggs and young fish. And then there's water lettuce, which sounds like something you would get in an exotic salad at one of those trendy farm-to-table foodie restaurants. While it sounds harmless enough, it grows in dense mats and can shade out native aquatic plants that are important as food for ducks and protection for young fish. The aquatic plant was at one time sold in backyard-pond supply stores nationwide, including in the Great Lakes states. Invasive-species experts say that water lettuce is not yet in the Great Lakes, but it might as well be since it's in Lake St. Clair and the Detroit River, which are part of the Great Lakes system. Water lettuce is already a major problem in Hawaii, where it chokes streams and ponds.

These are just three little beasts that could eventually become part of the Great Lakes ecosystem, according to the Great Lakes Aquatic Nonindigenous Species Information System (GLANSIS), an online database developed by the National Oceanic and Atmospheric Administration. GLANSIS has fifty-three species on a watch list of organisms likely to invade the Great Lakes through current pathways. It's a pretty sobering list.

So where do we go from here?

Ask the people who live in the region what they want from the Great Lakes in the future, and you will likely get a variety of answers. They want good fishing. They want clean water to drink. They want water that's not carrying parasites that are going to make them sick. They want to be able to picnic on the shoreline without having to smell rotting sewage or dead animals. They want to swim and boat in the water without having to worry about getting bogged down in slimy weeds. They want simple beauty.

Those sound like simple and achievable desires, but it starts to get complicated because the people of the region have differing perceptions of what the Great Lakes are today. For better or for worse, we tend to base those perceptions of the ecosystem's health on our memories of what the lakes were like years ago. Maybe we thought the Great Lakes were better back then because there were more fish to catch. Or maybe we think the ecosystem is healthier today because the water is clearer.

But most people living in the Great Lakes region don't realize that we humans have been manipulating the Great Lakes for decades. As much as we would like to believe these bodies of water are a self-regulating gift from nature, the Great Lakes are highly managed. We humans manipulate water levels to help shipping and pleasure boaters. We choose which species will be winners and which will be losers on the basis of economics when we stock fish for the benefit of a constituency.

Manipulating the lakes to maximize their benefits is both difficult and complicated, and it's only going to get harder in the future because of invasive species. That's partially because the Great Lakes are far different from what they were prior to the invasion of the zebra mussel and round goby or even the sea lamprey and alewife. The chemistry and nutrient flow of the lakes have been changed, and the food web has been dramatically altered. The plankton population has been dramatically reduced. The nutrient cycle is different. Native ciscoes are nearly gone. The whitefish population has plummeted and is not likely to recover anytime soon. The round goby has become the most important fish in the food web because it is now the most abundant feeder fish for large predators such as lake trout, walleyes, and other fish we like to catch.

The current trend is worrisome to Becky Cudmore of Fisheries and Oceans Canada because she believes that maintaining the lakes' biodiversity is the key to protecting them. The more homogenized the lakes get, Cudmore says, the less likely they will be able to withstand future invasions.

So having a plan going forward—developing strategies to maximize results—is a key first step in managing the lakes in the future. But what will that plan be? Do we manage for a few key species? Do we try to protect a few critical areas like spawning reefs or shoreline marshes? Do we try to reduce algal blooms? Is water quality the top issue?

Measuring the health of the Great Lakes in the Age of the Invasive is a more difficult prospect because we need a measure to judge against—a baseline. Do we judge the health of the Great Lakes going forward against what it was prior to the arrival of the zebra mussel or before the sea lamprey was established? Do we judge it against what we imagine the lakes looked like prior to European settlement? Or do we decide we're going to use the current state of the Great Lakes ecosystem as our new baseline? If we do, does that mean we are essentially throwing in the towel and tacitly accepting all the nonnative species that are now part of the ecosystem?

Some of those measures have already been developed jointly by Environment Canada and the US Environmental Protection Agency and are published every two years in the "State of the Great Lakes" report.[1] That report measures the health of the Great Lakes on the basis of several different indicators—fish populations, the levels of nutrients and toxins, the amount of contaminants in fish and waterfowl, the populations of *Diporeia*, and the health of coastal plants and amphibians, for example. For all these metrics, the impacts of invasives are best registered in the *Diporeia* and prey-fish populations. Both indicators show that four of the five Great Lakes are under increasing stress, with Lake Superior being the exception.

Because Lake Superior is relatively healthy and relatively unaffected by invasive species, some experts believe that it should be used as the baseline for the other lakes. But if the goal is to have all the lakes resemble Superior in the future, Mike Hoff of the US Fish and Wildlife Service cautions that each lake will have to have a different way to measure its health.

Overall, Hoff would measure success by looking at a few key components:

- Maintaining the sea lamprey population at a certain level.

- Ensuring lake trout reproduction in all five lakes.

- Addressing the lakes' needs from a top-down approach. By that, he means identifying the top-five predators in each lake and then identifying their key prey. If we can restore the prey—and the organisms they rely on—predators will take care of themselves.

Before making new management decisions about the Great Lakes, however, some biologists believe they need to get a better understanding of the native species and their relationships to the other organisms around them. "It is still astonishing to me how little research effort has been devoted to the Great Lakes," says David Lodge of the University of Notre Dame. "There has been so little sustained effort of biological monitoring in the Great Lakes. We have no idea what lives there now and what lived there in the past."

Lodge says a graduate student asked him a basic question about Great Lakes crayfish, but he couldn't answer it because no one had ever researched it. "We have a good handle on fish populations because of their value to humans, but biologists still don't have a good handle on all the organisms living in the ecosystem, particularly the ones at the benthic level," Lodge says.

Reuben Keller of Loyola University Chicago says that before we restore the Great Lakes, it's important that people who live in the Great Lakes region understand what has been lost. "The lakes are a different ecosystem from what they were prior to the commercial fishing," Keller says. "In a lot of ways, we are a lot poorer for it."

Keller points to the huge numbers of fish taken out of the lakes by commercial fishermen in the early twentieth century. Those records tell you that the abundance of fish used to be orders of magnitudes greater than it is now. "The Great Lakes used to be a much more productive, much richer place," Keller says. "We don't have a concept of what it was like years ago—it was common for people to catch seven-foot sturgeon. The idea that that was common is just stunning."

Despite the challenges, Norman Yan of York University in Toronto thinks we humans are up to the challenge of managing the Great Lakes into the future. "I tend to be an optimist about environmental problems," Yan says. "We've done not badly on many of these problems. People are saying the same thing today about invasives that people were saying about acid rain in the 1970s. We've solved [many environmental] problems. Invasives may not be as preventable as acid rain, but there are still things we can do.

"Humans have done a very good job of driving species to extinction," Yan says. "We need to figure out ways to drive these particular species to extinction."

It's the human penchant for short-term thinking that concerns Ryan Thum, the molecular biologist at Montana State University. Thum fears that people and policy makers will conclude that an ongoing battle against aquatic invasive species is so expensive and difficult, they will simply give up. "I'm worried that people will just throw up their hands and say we're going to live with it," Thum says.

Despite decades of damage, there is good reason to be optimistic about the future of the Great Lakes. We have made progress in shutting off pathways and reducing risks, but the threat of the Asian carps presents an opportunity to help protect the Great Lakes—a chance to mold public opinion in favor of additional control methods. "In the carp, could you ask for a better organism to raise the profile [of invasive species]? Round goby? Who cares? But these things? Wow!" says Phil Moy, the biologist who helped to design the barrier in the Chicago Sanitary and Ship Canal. "There's lots of interest in stopping the Asian carp. In the end, that's going to help for other stuff, too."

The Great Lakes, however, are not just about invasive carps and mussels; they're also about us as citizens of the region, because, ultimately, we will decide the future of the lakes and all the creatures within. Jon Allan, the director of Michigan's Office of the Great Lakes, says that everywhere he travels, he hears people tell him about how much they love the Great Lakes. He hears stories about fishing, swimming, sailing, picnicking—all kinds of outdoor experiences. But Allan is deeply concerned that if the people of the region don't continue to use our lakes because they've become so degraded, then our affinity with the lakes will also erode. And if our affinity with the lakes erodes, Allan says, so will our desire to care for them.

Even with the governors and premiers taking the lead, Allan believes ultimately the future of the Great Lakes will reflect the needs and desires of the people who live in the region. That's not to suggest that citizens storm the halls of their legislatures with torches and pitchforks, but our representatives need to know that nobody wants the Great Lakes to become an open sewer or even to return to the dumping grounds that they became in the middle of the twentieth century.

But we do have to ask ourselves difficult questions as part of a deep and lengthy public conversation: What do we want the Great Lakes to be in the age of invasive species? How much are we willing to spend to achieve our goals? Are we, the citizens of the region, willing to pay additional taxes to pay for research, prevention, and control? Given that these species can be controlled but likely never eradicated, how much control is enough?

Or do we just give up and live with it?

We as citizens should not abdicate our responsibilities to politicians or academics because, as Jon Allan says, the Great Lakes will ultimately reflect the will of the people. And they should. These lakes belong to all of us, and we have a duty to them and to ourselves to make sure they are both protected and improved. That means we can no longer stand on the side and passively let someone else make policy for us.

So the people of the region have to act now to ensure the future of the Great Lakes. We have decisions to make, individually and as a society, and what we do for these lakes today will be our legacy. That legacy will be written in water, but it will last for centuries. What do we want it to be?

# NOTES

## NOTES TO THE INTRODUCTION

1. Mark Brush, "Lake Erie Has 2% of the Water in the Great Lakes, but 50% of the Fish," Michigan Radio, November 5, 2013, http://michiganradio.org/post/lake-erie-has-2-water-great-lakes-50-fish.
2. Growing Blue, "Economic Impact of the Great Lakes: More than 1.5 Million Jobs, $62 Billion in Wages Directly Tied to Great Lakes," April 4, 2011, http://growing-blue.com/case-studies/economic-impact-of-the-great-lakes/.
3. David Lodge and David Finnoff, "Annual Losses to Great Lakes Region by Ship-Borne Invasive Species at Least $200 Million," fact sheet, Center for Aquatic Conservation, University of Notre Dame, Notre Dame, IN, 2008.

## NOTES TO CHAPTER 1

1. Peter L. Bernstein, *Wedding of the Waters: The Erie Canal and the Making of a Great Nation* (New York: Norton, 2005), 311.
2. The land between the Maumee and Wabash Rivers has risen, separating the two. However, Asian carps have made their way up the Wabash, and it would be possible for them to cross into the Maumee River and make their way into the Great Lakes if the rivers were ever joined again by severe flooding.
3. Irony alert: Once the land rose, the flow of the Chicago River was reversed so that water flowed toward Lake Michigan. In 1900, an engineering project reversed the flow of the river so that water would flow inland toward the Mississippi once again. It was done to prevent raw sewage from the city of Chicago from flowing into the city's drinking-water intake system. Sorry, St. Louis.
4. Glacial rebound is still occurring in the Great Lakes basin. The town of Superior, Wisconsin, rises approximately one-half inch each year, and the north shore of Lake Huron rises almost two inches a year.
5. F. Daniel Larkin, "Essay about the Erie Canal: Erie Canal Freight," in *Erie Canal Time Machine*, New York State Archives, www.archives.nysed.gov/projects/eriecanal/essays/ec_larkin4.shtml (accessed October 24, 2013).

6. Howard A. Tanner and Wayne H. Tody, "History of the Great Lakes Salmon Fishery: A Michigan Perspective," in *Sustaining North American Salmon: Perspectives across Regions and Disciplines*, ed. Kristine D. Lynch, M. L. Jones, and William W. Taylor (Bethesda, MD: American Fisheries Society, 2002), 141.

## NOTES TO CHAPTER 2

1. P. Fuller, L. Nico, E. Maynard, J. Larson, and A. Fusaro, "*Petromyzon marinus*," revised March 8, 2012, USGS Nonindigenous Aquatic Species Database, Gainesville, FL, http://nas.er.usgs.gov/queries/factsheet.aspx?SpeciesID=836.

2. Great Lakes Fishery Commission, "Sea Lamprey: A Great Lakes Invader," fact sheet 3, 2000, www.seagrant.umn.edu/downloads/x106.pdf.

3. US Geological Survey Upper Midwest Environmental Science Center, "Invasive Species: Sea Lamprey," last modified March 13, 2014, www.umesc.usgs.gov/invasive_species/sea_lamprey.html.

4. Jim Nies, "Water Levels and Flows," FLOW, http://flowforwater.org/issues/water-levels-and-flows/ (accessed November 21, 2013).

5. Jeramiah J. Smith, Shigehiro Kuraku, Carson Holt, Tatjana Sauka-Spengler, Ning Jiang, Michael S. Campbell, Mark D. Yandell, et al., "Sequencing of the Sea Lamprey (Petromyzon marinus) Genome Provides Insights into Vertebrate Evolution," *Nature Genetics* 45, no. 4 (2013): 415–21.

6. George Heath, Darcy Childs, Margaret F. Docker, David W. McCauley, and Steven Whyard, "RNA Interference Technology to Control Pest Sea Lampreys—A Proof-of-Concept," *PloS One* 9, no. 2 (2014): e88387.

7. Jeff Alexander, "Alewife Invasion," in *Pandora's Locks: The Opening of the Great Lakes–St. Lawrence Seaway* (East Lansing: Michigan State University Press, 2009).

8. "Alewife Explosion," *Time*, July 7, 1967, 66.

9. Howard A. Tanner and Wayne H. Tody, "History of the Great Lakes Salmon Fishery: A Michigan Perspective," in *Sustaining North American Salmon: Perspectives across Regions and Disciplines*, ed. Kristine D. Lynch, M. L. Jones, and William W. Taylor (Bethesda, MD: American Fisheries Society, 2002), 139–53.

## NOTES TO CHAPTER 3

1. Leslie Roberts, "Zebra Mussel Invasion Threatens US Waters," *Science* 249, no. 4975 (1990): 1370–72.

2. Darcy Henton, "Ottawa Ignored Zebra Mussel Warning, Scientist Says," *Toronto Star*, October 2, 1989.

3. Sarah A. Bailey, Matthew G. Deneau, Laurent Jean, Chris J. Wiley, Brian Leung, and Hugh J. MacIsaac, "Evaluating Efficacy of an Environmental Policy to Prevent Biological Invasions," *Environmental Science & Technology* 45, no. 7 (2011): 2554–61.

4. The National Invasive Species Act expired in 2002 after Congress failed to pass a reauthorization.

5. Tim Anderson, "US House Passes Bill Stripping States of Authority to Regulate Ballast Water Discharges," Council of State Governments, November 2011, www.csgmidwest.org/policyresearch/1111ballastwater.aspx.

6. Great Lakes Commission, "Status of Ballast Water Discharge Regulations in the Great Lakes Region," May 23, 2013, www.greatshipsinitiative.org/GLC_BW_Summary_2013.pdf.

7. A downloadable spreadsheet on the status of IMO conventions, including the 2004 ballast-water convention, is available at www.imo.org/About/Conventions/StatusOfConventions/Pages/Default.aspx.

8. Adam Lampert, Alan Hastings, Edwin D. Grosholz, Sunny L. Jardine, and James N. Sanchirico, "Optimal Approaches for Balancing Invasive Species Eradication and Endangered Species Management," *Science* 344, no. 6187 (2014): 1028–31.

## NOTES TO CHAPTER 4

1. Lyubov E. Burlakova, Alexander Y. Karatayev, Christopher Pennuto, and Christine Mayer, "Changes in Lake Erie Benthos over the Last 50 Years: Historical Perspectives, Current Status, and Main Drivers," *Journal of Great Lakes Research* 40, no. 3 (2014): 560–73.

2. Lee Bergquist, "Study: Invasive Zebra Mussels Improve Water Clarity in Great Lakes," Freep.com, April 4, 2014, www.freep.com/article/20140404/NEWS06/304040113/Study-Invasive-zebra-mussels-improve-water-clarity-Great-Lakes.

3. James T. Carlton, "The Zebra Mussel (Dreissena polymorpha) Found in North America in 1986 and 1987," *Journal of Great Lakes Research* 34, no. 4 (2008): 770–73.

4. Kelly Smith, "New Beer Brewed with Lake Minnetonka Zebra Mussels, Milfoil," *Star Tribune*, November 21, 2014.

5. David F. Reid and Dean Wilkinson, "Catalyst for Change: 'The Little Dreissenid That Did' (Change National Policy on Aquatic Invasive Species," in *Quagga and Zebra Mussels: Biology, Impacts, and Control*, 2nd ed., ed. Thomas F. Nalepa and Don W. Schloesser (Boca Raton, FL: CRC, 2014), 177–84.

## NOTES TO CHAPTER 5

1. W. T. Momot, "Crayfish Production: A Reflection of Community Energetics," *Journal of Crustacean Biology* 4 (1984): 35–54.

2. C. L. Hein, M. J. Vander Zanden, and J. J. Magnuson, "Intensive Trapping and Increased Fish Predation Cause Massive Population Decline of an Invasive Crayfish," *Freshwater Biology* 52 (2007): 1134–46.

3. Jeff Gunderson, "A Craving for Crayfish: Minnesota Discovers a Louisiana Tradition," Minnesota Sea Grant, 2008, www.seagrant.umn.edu/fisheries/craving_for_crayfish.

## NOTES TO CHAPTER 6

1. Habitattitude is a joint effort of the Pet Industry Joint Advisory Council, the US Fish and Wildlife Service, and the National Oceanic and Atmospheric Administration's Sea Grant program that is designed to help protect US ecosystems from the impacts of unwanted pets and to help pet owners find ways to dispose of their pets without releasing them into the wild. The campaign urges pet owners to find

responsible disposal methods, such as selling them to a pet store; donating them to a friend, a local aquarium, or a school; or euthanizing the animal.

2. Andrew R. Mahon, Lucas R. Nathan, and Christopher L. Jerde, "Meta-genomic Surveillance of Invasive Species in the Bait Trade," *Conservation Genetics Resources*, May 2014, 1–5.

3. Chris Halliday, "Credit Valley Conservation Bans Baitfish Use on Its Lands," *Caledon Enterprise*, August 13, 2014.

## NOTES TO CHAPTER 7

1. Southern Regional Aquaculture Center, "Using Grass Carp Fact Sheet," pub. no. 3600, 2002.

2. Dan Eagan, "Fishing for the Bottom Line: Sellers Seek Opportunity in Rivers Teeming with Carp," *Milwaukee Journal Sentinel*, October 16, 2006.

3. Anita M. Kelly, Carole R. Engle, Michael L. Armstrong, Mike Freeze, and Andrew J. Mitchell, "History of Introductions and Governmental Involvement in Promoting the Use of Grass, Silver, and Bighead Carps," in *Invasive Asian Carps in North America*, American Fisheries Society Symposium 74, ed. Duane C. Chapman and Michael H. Hoff (Bethesda, MD: American Fisheries Society, 2011), 163–74.

4. L. G. Nico and M. E. Neilson, "*Mylopharyngodon piceus*," revised March 15, 2012, USGS Nonindigenous Aquatic Species Database, Gainesville, FL, http://nas.er.usgs.gov/queries/factsheet.aspx?SpeciesID=573.

5. Kelly et al., "History of Introductions and Governmental Involvement," 1.

6. Morgan Shelburne, "Walleye and Perch Vulnerable If Bighead and Silver Carp Enter Great Lakes," *Petoskey News*, November 8, 2013, www.petoskeynews.com/news/local/walleye-and-perch-vulnerabl...enter/article_7da5e082-4879-11e3-bb7d-0014bcf6878.html?mode=print.

7. Greg G. Sass, Collin Hinz, Anthony C. Erickson, Nerissa N. McClelland, Michael A. McClelland, and John M. Epifanio, "Invasive Bighead and Silver Carp Effects on Zooplankton Communities in the Illinois River, Illinois, USA," *Journal of Great Lakes Research* 40, no. 4 (2014): 911–21, www.sciencedirect.com/science/article/pii/S0380133014001798.

8. Chuck Quirmbach, "Great Lakes Fish on a Diet," Michigan Radio, October 2, 2013, http://michiganradio.org/post/great-lakes-fish-diet#stream/0.

9. US Army Corps of Engineers Chicago District, "Summary of Fish-Barge Interaction Research and Fixed Dual Frequency Identification Sonar (DIDSON) Sampling at the Electric Dispersal Barrier in Chicago Sanitary and Ship Canal," release no. 122013-001, December 20, 2013.

10. Francis M. Veraldi, Kelly Baerwaldt, Brook Herman, Shawna Herleth-King, Matthew Shanks, Len Kring, and Andrew Hannes, "Non-native Species of Concern and Dispersal Risk for the Great Lakes and Mississippi," Great Lakes and Mississippi River Interbasin Study, September 16, 2011, http://glmris.anl.gov/documents/docs/Non-Native_Species.pdf.

11. Great Lakes Commission, "Evaluation of Physical Separation Alternatives for the Great Lakes and Mississippi River Basins in the Chicago Area Waterway System," January 25, 2012, http://projects.glc.org/caws/pdf/FINALHDRREPORT12512.pdf.

12. State of Michigan, et al., and Grand Traverse Band of Ottawa and Chippewa Indians, v. United States Army Corps of Engineers and Metropolitan Water Reclamation District of Greater Chicago, No. 10C4457 (N.D. Ill. December 3, 2012).

13. State of Michigan, et al., and Grand Traverse Band of Ottawa and Chippewa Indians, v. United States Army Corps of Engineers and Metropolitan Water Reclamation District of Greater Chicago (7th Cir. July 14, 2014), http://media.ca7.uscourts.gov/cgi-bin/rssExec.pl?Submit=Display&Path=Y2014/D07-14/C:12-3800:J:Wood:aut:T:f nOp:N:1380188:S:0.

14. Tina Lam, "Asian Carp: US as Much to Blame as Fish Farms for Escape," *Detroit Free Press*, July 20, 2011.

15. Tad W. Locher and James T. Lamer, "Analysis of Blue Catfish (Ictalurus Furcatus) Gut Contents: An Assessment of Feeding Adaptation in Response to Asian Carp Invasion in the Mississippi River Basin," *Proceedings of the Mississippi River Research Consortium* 46 (April 2014), http://m-r-r-c.org/2014/2014%20MRRC%20Program_4-11-14.pdf.

16. Fisheries and Oceans Canada, Canadian Science Advisory Secretariat, "Binational Ecological Risk Assessment of Bigheaded Carps (Hypophthalmichthys spp.) for the Great Lakes Basin," Science Advisory Report 2011/071, July 2012, www.dfo-mpo.gc.ca/csas-sccs/Publications/SAR-AS/2011/2011_071-eng.pdf.

17. US Fish and Wildlife Service, TGC Inspection and Certification Program, www.fws.gov/warmsprings/fishhealth/frgrscrp.html (accessed December 16, 2014).

## NOTES TO CHAPTER 8

1. Ecological Society of America, "Controlling Invasive Species: How Effective Is the Lacey Act?," *ScienceDaily*, September 13, 2007, www.sciencedaily.com/releases/2007/09/070910163257.htm.

2. Defenders of Wildlife, "Broken Screens: The Regulation of Live Animal Imports in the United States," August 1, 2007, www.defenders.org/publications/broken_screens_report.pdf.

## NOTES TO THE CONCLUSION

1. More information is available at www.epa.gov/solec/.

# INDEX

*Page numbers in italics refer to illustrations*